Instruments ot Christ's Love

The Ministry of Readers

Sally Buck
Graham Dodds
Phillip Tovey

scm press

Published in 2016 by SCM Press
Editorial office
3rd Floor, Invicta House,
108–114 Golden Lane,
London EC1Y 0TG, UK

SCM Press is an imprint of Hymns Ancient & Modern Ltd
(a registered charity)
13A Hellesdon Park Road, Norwich,
Norfolk NR6 5DR, UK
www.scmpress.co.uk

British Library Cataloguing in Publication data

A catalogue record for this book is available
from the British Library

978 0 334 05435 1

Typeset by Manila Typesetting Company
Printed and bound by CPI Group (UK) Ltd, Croydon

Contents

Introduction

The year 2016 marks the official 150th birthday of Reader ministry in the Church of England. This factor inspired the writing of this book, although its contents are in no way limited to this anniversary. In one way the book stands in a tradition of predecessors marking Reader anniversaries. Thus T. G. King wrote *Readers: A Pioneer Ministry*[1] at the centenary and Rhoda Hiscox *Celebrating Reader Ministry*[2] at the 125th celebrations. This book continues in that tradition but also adds to the small but important collection of works considering the role of Readers. This would include Gordon Kuhrt and Pat Nappin, *Bridging the Gap*,[3] Cathy Rowling and Paula Gooder, *Reader Ministry Explored*[4] and Charles Read and Phillip Tovey, *Reader Ministry Today*.[5] Alongside could be put an intermittent series of church assembly and synod reports finishing with *Reader Upbeat*.[6] Compared to the concentration of literature on the priesthood this is a modest collection, and perhaps celebrating anniversaries is a good antidote to the forgetfulness around this ministry.

Reader ministry is a somewhat neglected area considering that in the present Church of England, the number of Readers is roughly equivalent to the number of incumbents. Within the Church this is a large and significant ministry that is often under-resourced, underappreciated and yet absolutely necessary. Indeed, Reader ministry has shown itself to be a flexible and Spirit-led ministry, continually renewing as the needs of the Church are changing to fit the evolving ministerial context.

It is a conviction of the authors of this book that Readers are an underused resource and yet are motivated and excellent people equipped by the Spirit for lay ministry in the Church. All the authors work in one way or another with Readers, although Sally Buck is presently the only Reader, the other two authors being priests.

Part of the problem in the present Church is a rather negative perception of Readers. They are often seen as mini-vicars in blue scarves who don't do the job as well as the vicar but are needed to be there as a stopgap. They can be seen as a ministry that lacks any theological underpinning. They are also sometimes seen as wanting to support 'traditional Church' and 'keeping the system going' rather than being interested in 'emerging Church' and where God is leading. It is ironic that T. G. King called readers a 'pioneer ministry', not using technical language as we would today but perhaps challenging the assumption that Readers cannot be pioneering. The authors would like to challenge this assumption as simply not representing the experience we have in the diversity of Reader ministry. God continues to call a great company of people to be bearers of his good news on behalf the Church, and they are found in an extraordinary variety of ministries. Rather than want to tighten the job description of Readers, we rejoice in this diversity.

We start the book with a couple of chapters looking at the theology of Reader ministry. Sally Buck begins with a theology from the bottom up, starting with the stories of Readers and interpreting these through a new monastic lens with a view to mission today. Phillip Tovey has a more traditional theological chapter relating the ministry of all the baptized to that of canonically commissioned ministers, in the light of the work of John Collins on *diakonia*. With another chapter from Sally Buck we then look at the variety of ministry by deliberately focusing on Readers whose ministry is outside of the Church. Then Phillip Tovey looks backwards in history, showing some of the pioneering in which Readers were involved, particularly in the American colonies. As such he wishes to change the history books, showing that the Church of England had Readers from 1706 but that most of them were overseas. The pioneering spirit is taken up once again by Graham Dodds, who suggests that Readers can be and are involved in pioneer ministry and that this is something to foster.

We see this book as a beginning not an end: a beginning to further discussion about lay ministry and lay ministries; a beginning to a richer theology of ministry that includes all ministries; a beginning of a change in perception of the nature of Readers; and a beginning, or more really a continuation, of a pioneering role for Readers ministering in the world. Often Readers are seen as a problem: What do we do with Readers? How do we understand what they are? These are the wrong questions. Rather we should ask: How can we best deploy a group of laypeople who are enthusiastic for ministry and have been trained to use their gifts as God has given them? We offer this book in celebration of Readers.

Notes

1 T. G. King, 1973, *Readers: A Pioneer Ministry*, London: Myland Fund.
2 R. Hiscox, 1991, *Celebrating Reader Ministry*, London: Mowbray.
3 G. W. Kuhrt and P. Nappin, 2002, *Bridging the Gap: Reader Ministry Today*, London: Church House Publishing.
4 C. Rowling and P. Gooder, 2009, *Reader Ministry Explored*, London: SPCK.
5 C. Read and P. Tovey, 2010, *Reader Ministry Today*, Grove Worship Series 203, Cambridge: Grove Books.
6 Ministry Division of the Archbishops' Council, 2009, *Reader Upbeat: Revised Report*, www.readers.cofe.anglican.org/u_d_lib_pub/p112.pdf.

I

Ministers of Word

SALLY BUCK

What's vocational for me
is the whole thing about ministry of word
it's about crafting words.[1]

This chapter aims to focus on ministry of the Word, one aspect of Reader ministry. Ministry of word is often interpreted as a liturgical role. Services of the Word, including morning and evening prayer, are often led by Readers. Readers are also often involved in leading the first part of eucharistic services, including the calls to repentance and affirmation of faith, although their role is not clearly defined. While this can be considered to be an accurate interpretation of the phrase 'ministry of word' where Readers are concerned, I would suggest that it is an extremely limited one, and it is my intention in this chapter to suggest a more imaginative way of working with the description.

In the beginning was the Word

As identified elsewhere in this book, there is little published, well-developed thinking about Reader ministry from a theological perspective. I would like to suggest that Reader ministry can be considered in the light of a number of theological themes. It is possible to draw on the connection between the contemporary experiences of Readers exercising their ministry and the theological concept of Jesus as the Word, in a way that highlights the desire for the Word to be made known through Readers' ministry of word offered in many different settings. This chapter will provide the meeting place between these experiences and the resources of the Christian tradition in a way that highlights and celebrates the aspect of ministry identified by Readers as ministry of word.

This chapter also offers a theological reflection on this one aspect of Reader ministry, incorporating an interpretation of the concepts of 'sacred space' and 'theopoetics'. These terms and other concepts are offered as ways of illuminating and developing the wonderfully creative and insightful way that Readers have spoken with me about their experience as ministers of word. The words belong to those who took part in a recent research project. The participants' real names are not used, as was agreed at the outset of the project, but they know who they are and I wish to thank them for their generosity and enthusiasm and for agreeing that their words may be used. It is their words and their motivation that are worthy of recounting and celebrating. I simply aim to offer a framework within which they can speak for themselves. What is offered is for you to consider with an open heart and mind. Some of it will resonate with you and some will not, but all of it reflects the passion and motivation of a number of people who are wholeheartedly serving God in the Church and the world by offering their gift of wordsmithing with the intention of this gifting being used for the common good.

Let me begin with my own story, which is intrinsically one of identifying myself as having a ministry of word even before I had any concept of Reader ministry. As a baptized Christian my work environment was an offering of my gifts and skills. I trained as a speech and language therapist and later as a counsellor. As such I was working with words as part of the healing process for people who had often experienced significant medical, accidental or emotional trauma. In these roles I became increasingly aware of the power of language to hurt and heal.

As a result of my later sense of vocation to Reader ministry, which was a way of offering my own ministry of word to be more formally exercised within the context of the Anglican Church, I developed a rather expansive understanding of the idea of ministry of word.

It is possible to consider a Reader's ministry of word as being associated simply with a liturgical ministry, a preaching and teaching role. Alternatively, as I have come to understand it in my own life, it is possible to consider the gifting and vocation associated with ministry of word as being related to the whole of life. The research project has highlighted for me that many Readers describe themselves first and foremost as ministers of word. What they mean by this varies significantly. I have, though, been greatly impressed by the qualities of observation and crafting of words exhibited by those involved in the practice of ministry of word. In particular the stories shared with me have helped me to develop an awareness of how moments of encounter with God are experienced through ministry of word; times when our words meet the Word. It is my hope in this chapter to consider the riches that are contained in this aspect of Reader ministry, to engage with some of the literature that has informed my thinking and to give voice to those who have so generously shared their sense of identity with me.

One of the words that came up over and over again when I spoke to Readers was 'craft'. There were many expressions of wordsmithing, crafting of words and even playing with words, all of which were related to every aspect of ministry, from preaching and teaching and preparing intercessions, to conversations with work colleagues and incidental meetings with others. Much of the language used reflects the need to pay attention to the world around, to biblical texts and to what others are saying. It is also acknowledged as being of considerable importance for those with a ministry of word to know when not to use any

words. Silence and phrasing are given almost as much importance as the actual choice of words.

Given this emphasis on crafting of words and the spaces between
words, I would like to suggest that there is something poetic about
ministry of word. While most Readers would not call themselves
poets, they are employing poetic process in much that they do in
the routine acts of ministry. This leads to the possibility of a theopoetic expression of ministry of word, which celebrates not only
the practicalities of using words in liturgical and pastoral settings
but also the artisan nature of the craft of the Reader.

Leech claims that 'Poetry is theology leaping out of the file
cabinet and into the heart . . . the Word or words that stir our
souls' and 'A poet is a poet because, like Jesus, she sees what
is really there.'[2] Many Readers identify their layness as being a
call to represent the world to the Church. Seeing the world as it
really is becomes important if this view is to be sustained.

Theopoetics, as defined by Wilder, is 'a crafting of words which
results in the shaping (*poiein*) of an experience of the divine (*theo*)'.[3]
While there are many more definitions and usages of the word from
the perspectives of literary and biblical criticism, it is this definition
that contributes most helpfully to a consideration of the craft of
ministry which, through careful use of words, shapes an experience
of the divine. Working with this definition as a possible theological
framework for ministry of word as practised by Readers emphasizes both the crafting aspect of the ministry and also the desire
to use words to bring people closer to God. It might be possible
to state this as the desire to work with words in a way that helps to
create interpersonal sacred space.

In order to focus thinking about how Reader ministry might be
related to the creation of sacred space, it is helpful to consider the
work of George Lings. Writing in the series Encounters on the Edge
in 2009, Lings identifies seven sacred spaces found consistently in
historic monasticism. He suggests that they are also of importance
to the new monastic movement.[4] These spaces are based on the

architecture and purpose of the original monasteries but the concepts have been developed to relate to the new monastic communities of today. These communities are often dispersed in nature and so the way the sacred spaces are considered is not bound by a building but does have its roots in the physical space occupied and the rules lived out by the early monastic communities. While most Readers will not be called to such a specific ministry, either in residential or dispersed communities of traditional or new monastic nature, I would like to suggest that these seven sacred spaces can help us to consider the spaces in which Readers' identified ministries of word are exercised. With a raised level of awareness of these spaces and of the significance of the ministry of word both in Church and the world, Readers are well placed to offer wisdom and guidance. In what follows I am using Lings' work as a lens through which to consider the extent to which Readers' ministry of word might be intentionally offered into each of the areas of life of the various communities of which they are a part, both church-based and beyond.

Lings' spaces will be considered and then Readers' own words will serve to illuminate the extent to which ministry might be offered in each of these areas of life. The words are presented as poetic stanzas. This is how they were captured from the interviews and they are presented in this form to allow the emphasis and the phrasing – and on occasion the pauses – to be heard. While this is not intended to be poetry in a carefully crafted and honed sense, to create prose from these words would be for me to inject too much interpretation and for the words to lose their potency. Those who shared with me thought carefully and deeply. The number of times the sense of crafting both words and silences was referred to makes it essential that their care with the spoken word be reflected in its representation as written word.

What is quoted comes from the heart. The motivation of all whose words form and inform this chapter can, I think, be summed up by the idea that Reader ministry is:

Not a job
A vocation
to break open the word
The word that is
as Christ was the Word

There's a
Sacred responsibility
to break open the word
Reader responsibility
to be
Sacred
Holy
Word-breakers[5]

and that in everything there is the calling to:

Make words meaningful
Let them live
Let them breathe
creating

Sacred space
Here
and now
and everywhere[6]

Cell

The first sacred space identified by Lings is that of the cell.[7] The cell is the place of personal encounter with God. It is a place to be alone with God, to allow God to speak and also a place of rest and sleep.

Encounter the sacred
Leave with a sense
of numinous[8]

These words refer to time spent with God, whether in church or in personal prayer. To engage in a ministry of word requires intentional and dedicated encounter with the sacred, and Readers are often very aware of their own need for space in which to listen to God.

This encounter, Leo believes, is with our:

Unchanging
Faithful
God
whose compassions fail not

Many reasons are given for making time and space to be with God but they are summed up in the idea that we are:

Making space
For the Word
To take root[9]

There is a real sense that Readers are responding to a call to:

Listen
In the world
Of the world
But listening to the Word
and bringing the two
Together

This can only be done if time is given to listening 'to the Word'; a characteristic of time in the cell.

> Silence and space
> Are essential to ministry
> We're too busy with words
> Value silence
> And space
> That's where it goes deep
> Space to allow the Holy Spirit in
>
> And then apply it
> Find your calling's outworking[10]

It is arguably only in the finding of space – silent, cell-like sacred space – that the beginnings of the 'calling's outworking' will be found.

> Reader ministry
> As a kind of expression
> of longing
> God's longing for us
> Our longing for God[11]

Chapel

Lings' second sacred space is that of chapel. This is the public sacred space in contrast to the privacy of the cell. Arguably the chapel is the sacred space most often thought of when considering the outworking of Reader ministry, but Lings' comment that 'the art is living truly with God in both places and co-operating with what they do differently'[12] is important and is reflected in the number of times Readers spoke with me about the need for silence and contemplation before taking part in public worship.

Public worship, and especially preaching, was spoken of with great passion and fondness. While I am aware of a number of Readers who feel that the liturgy and intercessions are their particular gifting within the church setting, a celebration of Reader ministry would seem to be lacking if it did not concentrate on these wonderful expressions relating to preaching.

This is where the poetic processes referred to earlier seem to be most significant. The poet crafts words, offering an interpretation of the world to her or his readers with the knowledge that those words may be interpreted in quite different ways by those hearing or reading them. There is something of a vulnerability about the poetic art that is also present in the art of the preacher. Like the creation of a poem, the crafting of a sermon is not always experienced as easy. There is struggle with God and self in the process and the delivery.

It is up to the preacher to:

Cast seeds on the lawn
See how they're picked up

Making space
For the word
To take root

We have to
Lead worship
Understand the Church's language
Have a biblical foundation
Have that formality

Liturgy is part of our toolkit
But our function is broader

Pitting myself against the Word
Jacob-like

> Wrestling a sermon into being
> Pitting myself against myself
> Lord take down my barriers
> Allow the Word to speak[13]

The concept of the Reader as a craftsperson, a wordsmith, is picked up in these words, which emphasize the lay role of the Reader as a positive one.

> Not just what you say
> but how you say it
>
> Lay preachers
> have time
>
> Mulling and sifting
> The craft of the wordsmith
> in preparation
> for preaching
>
> Preach to the head
> Preach to the heart
>
> Finding the key
> that will touch the heart
> That's what preaching offers
>
> Maybe it's in the pause
> The words unsaid
> God's spirit
> speaking to hearts
> In the gap
> The pause
> The silence[14]

The crafting of words is also expressed in the realization that preaching is more than, although akin to, teaching. Relating his realization of the need to become a storyteller to his experiences as a teacher, John says:

> I thought
> preaching
> if you say something
> and if you really want them to lap it up
> say it louder
> that that was it really.
> I've only just learnt
> that isn't so
>
> The greatest thing I ever heard
> So simple
> I do what Jesus did
> I tell stories[15]

Telling stories about faith and everyday life employs linguistic images in a way that is 'incremental in that they add to our understanding. We see more profoundly into reality through the truth of imagination than we do when we pursue the illusion of precise, specifiable, purely objective, literal description.'[16] By seeking to observe their surroundings and then telling stories that relate these observations to faith, Readers who choose to preach in this way are taking part, through the use of metaphor, symbol and myth, in what Avis would identify as 'a penetration of reality [that] is heuristic, not definitive; it is fragmentary, not total; it leaves the ocean of being largely unexplored'.[17] As with the poet, words are offered and a direction set, but the ultimate meaning-making process will be between the hearer and the Spirit.

What is being produced by the crafting of words, whether in the production of a sermon or in any other setting, is not a product that is handmade and either useful or ornamental in a concrete sense. A number of Readers did, however, speak of wordsmithing in language that suggested something of an artisan nature being embodied in their craft. Crafting, honing and working were regularly used words. In the words that follow, the desire to create something of great quality, something that points to God, from the everyday, ordinary situations and words to hand, suggests to me the attitude of the artisan craftsperson who skilfully uses the tools they have collected to create something of quality from everyday materials.

A precious stone
crafted offering
light
skill
value

The process of distilling
is important
Whisky is distilled
Water is distilled
Thoughts distilled
and words given life

Always keeping my tools handy
pen and paper by my bed
A wordsmith
Ready
Prepared
Inspired

I put words around
things
Dandelion seeds
On the updraft
Like Hopkins
Open up meaning
without horizon
from the little tiny
world visions

Find in the minutely ordinary
the glory of God[18]

'Poetic practitioners will often speak about the experience, in the composition of poetry, of listening, of being taken aback by what is heard and then said. And the poetry that results may set out to reconstruct perception as if things were indeed being seen anew.'[19] Williams' words seem to echo some of the sentiments expressed by Readers speaking of their crafting of words when preparing to preach. 'Opening up meaning without horizon from the little tiny world visions', 'distilling', 'mulling' and desiring a reaction from the hearers all suggest a desire to 'reconstruct perception as if things were indeed being seen anew'. The Reader's involvement in the world and the skills of the wordsmith are so often combined to offer something significant within the sacred space of church or chapel; opening up new perspectives and new perceptions or, in the following words, helping people to say 'ah, yes'.

how great the prophets were
in using words
to help people to say
ah, I see.

word
poetry
words in a sermon
ought to help people to say
ah, yes[20]

One final thought on the topic of preaching. No one spoke about aiming to produce a 'nice sermon', although many did speak of a feeling of maybe not having hit the mark with a sermon that received these words from members of the congregation as they left church. The desire to bring about a reaction from those receiving the words offered in preaching was, however, a common theme expressed in these and many other words:

Love what I say
Hate what I say
No matter
But please react[21]

Chapter

Chapter is the third sacred space identified by Lings.[22] It is here that decisions are made. Chapter is 'more a social and governmental function than a specific building'. In church life many Readers are part of Parochial Church Councils. It is here that the decisions are made about much of what counts as community life within the church. Chapters are places of tension. Sometimes this tension is creative and energizing. At other times the tension can lead to frayed tempers and disagreements. Readers often speak of themselves as those whose ministry of word is expressed in their ability to interpret people to one another. Readers may, and often do, find themselves as go-betweens; as those who hold the tension in decision-making situations and who use their communication skills to enlighten and examine arguments.

Being licensed lay ministers offers freedom but also involves accountability, and this is expressed in a number of the recorded conversations. The fact that Readers are often people who have lived in their communities for many years and offer their ministry on a voluntary basis seems to heighten the sense of responsibility experienced by many.

Reader ministry
Between
On the edge
In the gaps
Between a rock and a hard place
In that overlapping place
A painful place sometimes
But interesting
Dynamic
Creative
That's the sort of place
Of Word ministry

Know your responsibility
And to whom you are accountable[23]

Responsibility to the world
as a minister of the Church
Licensed
Representation
Responsibility
To God, bishop, others
self[24]

In the promises made at admission to Reader ministry, all have promised obedience to their bishop 'in all things lawful and honest' and likewise to the minister in whose cure they serve.

They have also promised 'to endeavour, as far as in me lies, to promote peace and unity, and to conduct myself as becomes a worker for Christ, for the good of his Church, and for the spiritual welfare of all people'.[25] These are significant promises made in good faith and reflected in the seriousness with which Readers approach their role both inside and outside the chapter, where decisions are made that will potentially impact large numbers of people.

Within the decision-making processes there is an acknowledgment of the responsibility of those who minister in this way. Words are described as being able to 'shift and change',[26] and there is a need to be aware of the power that can be misused by those who enjoy 'playing with words'.[27] It is suggested that questions need to be asked on a regular basis:

Are they my words?
or His words?
Are they authentic?
Are they true?
How do you know you've got it right?[28]

These questions are relevant no matter where the ministry of word is being practised. If it is true that 'we have a sacred responsibility to encourage and illuminate all that is inherently good and special in each other',[29] then an awareness of the authenticity of our words and a constant reflexive questioning, as indicated by Monica's words above, would seem to be essential qualities of those who exercise a ministry of word.

Cloister

The fourth sacred space is the cloister. This is a place that offers shelter; from heat or rain, depending on the location of the monastic community.[30] Within this sheltered space, though, people wander and there are accidental and incidental meetings. Ministry of word cannot always be planned for. Readers are known in their communities. Maybe the cloister experience of those incidental meetings with others is more likely to be in the sheltered spaces of bus shelters and corner-shop queues than in a specifically set-aside area, but that does not make these meetings any less significant. It is possible to use words in a way that transforms any incidental meeting into one that is perceived as sacred; one in which God's presence is sensed.

It is again the skill of listening rather than speaking that is highlighted by Readers involved in the study. Being alongside people and having time to listen before responding, being able to find different words for different people and situations are considered to be important qualities when seeking to draw alongside others in what might be considered to be cloister spaces. Being those who have a public, representative ministry but who do not wear uniform of any kind is sometimes experienced as problematic. Those who minister as chaplains recall times when their ordained colleagues can enter a space and be instantly recognized, while Readers in the same or similar roles often take longer to build relationships before their role is acknowledged. However, this lack of instant recognition and lay identity are also recounted as part of the strength and the offering of the Reader. In the words that follow, all of these aspects of ministry of word in the incidental meeting places are expressed.

It's a listening
and a finding of language
Language that fits
Fits the person

Listening in the world

Anonymous Readers
Listen without being known
Merge into the crowds

Unlabelled
Unidentifiable
Hearing what's actually being said[31]

Put another way:

> My ordinariness
> challenges others
> To see differently[32]

Being a layperson, living most of life in work or in the local community, a Reader is often in a position to be having conversations about faith with people who may be reluctant to attend more formal church-led studies or services. It has often been my privilege to be approached in work staffrooms, or in my office if my door was open, by people who had questions about the meaning of life when they were experiencing challenges or significant life events. Being ready to answer these questions, in a way that encouraged further conversation, has always been both a challenge and a joy. While Marilyn was speaking of preaching when using the words that follow, it is also the case that the Ministry Division of the Church of England, in its outcomes for Readers in training, states that Readers should be able to preach the gospel both in church and outside of church.[33] With an 'evangelist's heart', it seems probable that Marilyn's idea of talking about Jesus is not limited to the holy space that is chapel but that all space is considered holy, and that speaking of Jesus is a natural process, whether in chapel or cloister or, in all likelihood, any other space that has the potential to become hallowed by prayer and faithful talk of Jesus (such as the post office queue or the doctor's waiting room?). Those words spoken by Marilyn are:

An evangelist's heart
Talking about Jesus
when opportunity presents

Grow from no faith
to deep faith
This is my desire
For others
For me

Keep it simple
Direct
Ordinary
The words will speak
for themselves

Know the phrase
Pray
Leave them with a thought
and a prayer[34]

The desire for all space to be experienced as sacred space was expressed on a number of occasions, but particularly in the following words, which I use to sum up the possibilities of ministry of word offered in those incidental and coincidental encounters in the spaces that may be called 'cloister':

The sacred within you
at all times
meets the sacred
in the other[35]

Garden

Garden as sacred space has a number of interpretations.[36] The monastic understanding of garden space was not the twenty-first-century hobby space but a place where physical work took place in order that food was produced for the refectory. Without the garden both life and diet would have been considered to be unbalanced. Readers' work may not always be physical and may not often be so directly related to physical sustenance, although one notable exception is that of Karin, who in Chapter 3 on world-facing ministries recounts her story of the growth of her allotment as a space of meeting with God, with others, and of provision (spiritual and physical). Whatever work is for most Readers, it certainly is the place where many identify life being balanced and all that is learnt and considered in other spaces coming together in life in the world. Work, in monastic communities, was considered to be essential. Considering the rules of monastic communities, Lings states that 'Opus Dei ["work of God"] is understood as work with mind, heart and hands . . . As such work is not just a weapon to avoid idleness; it is regarded as a friend to the soul.'[37] Readers' ministry of word extends to their work environments, both paid and voluntary employment, as they find God in the work itself and in those they work alongside. Often considered to be safe people to confide in, Readers recount significant experiences where work space has become sacred space.

Ruth speaks of times when being known as a Reader in the work environment has led to feelings of being:

> Seen for who you are
> Known as Christian
> Exposed – unclothed
> Open – vulnerable

This sense of vulnerability is significant but also leads to the expression of an awareness of the need to take care of others. Particularly, maybe, in the work environment where the Reader has been known for a number of years and may be in a professional position of authority over others, it is considered important to:

Be very careful
of your words
Use them wisely
Slowly[38]

The garden may be experienced as a place of work that involves craft and tools in a conscious and creative way with the intention of feeding others. Maybe that feeding will not be literal and physical in most Readers' work environments, but it will be intentional and will involve some hard work. I would suggest that this is what Monica is speaking of when she says:

Being users of words
Is a gifting
If you're good with words
You should use them
In the service of the Lord[39]

For others there will be a more direct correlation between professional work and the role of the Reader. Marilyn speaks of the environment of work as being that of training. This is a key example of someone whose professional life and their Reader vocation to be a preacher and teacher in the world overlap significantly. This is how this calling is expressed:

Training is my gifting
My ministry at work

My desire
To make a difference
A difference for God[40]

I have been struck by how many Readers come from the teaching and pastoral or medical professions. All of these backgrounds necessarily involve listening and communication skills. Readers are often utilizing the skills that they gain in the 'garden', the workplace, directly and indirectly in their ministerial roles. God's gifting is not limited to one or other environment.

Refectory

As might be expected, the refectory is the space that fulfils the roles of 'physical nourishing, social gathering, mutual serving and personal meeting'.[41] Lings claims that 'chapel has eclipsed many other legitimate functions that monasticism has unwittingly unearthed'[42] in the identification of what church is and might be. His suggestion that 'if we will start with the dynamics of refectory we shall be in a far better state to offer relational and authentic missional hospitality' speaks powerfully to those engaged in a lay ministry of word. Readers are in a position to offer such hospitality and to meet with others who are offering hospitality and to consider this a space in which our hospitality might be a place of using words and listening skills in a way that is missional. The ability to meet with a wide variety of people around many tables is spoken of by Monica. She expresses her joy at being in a position to:

listen
In the privileged position
Of sitting at such
Interesting tables[43]

While not many of those taking part in the study made direct reference to the opportunities offered by the refectory space, a number of Readers did recount the desire to be welcoming to the stranger, open and hospitable. Many conversations in churches take place over coffee and biscuits and the number of churches offering café-style worship is growing. Readers are often ideally placed to both offer and receive hospitality. The story of Martha and Mary shows us the importance of being able to both sit at Jesus' feet and to provide physical sustenance for those who are learning of God. The challenge of offering hospitality, according to Pohl, is to widen the circle of those who are invited beyond the acceptable and expected members of our congregations and groups. She claims that:

> when a person who is not valued by society is received by a socially respected person or group as a human being with dignity and worth, small transformations occur. When people are socially invisible, their needs and concerns are not acknowledged and no one even notices the injustices they suffer. Hospitality can begin a journey toward visibility and respect.[44]

Many Readers' ministry of word is missionally focused. The refectory, the place of hospitality, however it is embodied, can offer a space in which this missional focus can be truly transformational.

Scriptorium

The final sacred space identified by Lings is that of scriptorium; a place of study. Ongoing ministerial education formalizes the need for Readers to engage in lifelong learning. Those who see their ministry as one of word often relate an insatiable appetite for reading and learning. In monastic settings this study was not seen as an end in itself but was to be related to context and to encourage deepening of relationships with God. Readers often report learning and study as being in the service of others. While the learning itself is enjoyed, it is most often reported as being a way of improving communication in sermons and teaching environments.

How do we
Minister the word?
We preach

Formally

We teach
All sorts of people
All sorts of places[45]

Time in the scriptorium; time reading and studying to keep up with new developments and in order that the preacher is not aloof and distant but someone who preaches to 'the head and the heart' is seen as offering the necessary:

Challenge to grow
Change
Be transformed
Continually
To develop
and grow
To think
and respond[46]

The scriptorium is not only a place of learning but also of creativity. The beauty and quality of the decoration and illumination of the Lindisfarne Gospels is a prime example of the creative role of the scriptorium. Ministry of word can also be considered to be creative. This chapter has already made reference to the

possible poetic nature of ministry of word. Another creative interpretation of this ministry is offered in these words:

> Ministry of word is music
> Because music carries
> all sorts of things
> Like emotions
> and beauty
> and expressions
> and mystery
> It interprets
> It articulates something
> It can transport you
> It can challenge you
> And all of those things
> And I think our ministry
> of the word
> is a bit similar to that[47]

Creativity requires practice. If ministry of word is like any creative
art or craft, time in the scriptorium honing the skills will be essential.

Infirmary

A monastic space not included in Lings' list of sacred spaces
is that of the infirmary. It was acknowledged by those who
shared their stories with me that words can 'hurt and heal'[48]
but very little was said about ministry of word as a healing
ministry in itself. Maybe this is a possible conversation to
grow out of the insights shared so far in this chapter. Some
stories will be shared in Chapter 3 by those whose ministry
has been predominantly in chaplaincy settings; one in particular in the hospice movement. It is possible, though, that to
some extent all ministry of word has the potential to bring

about healing and reconciliation. When preparing to preach on the Bible passage telling the story of a woman who had experienced years of bleeding who was healed by secretly touching the hem of Jesus' cloak, Reader Naomi Smith wrote a poem, 'It was Just a Secret Touch' (extracts of which can be found below). This poem led to a group of Readers considering ways the lay ministry of word may also offer a secret touch to those among whom we live and minister: a touch that helps people to hear God calling them 'daughter' or 'son'; a touch that takes them further along the journey towards healing and wholeness.

> It was just a secret touch.
> No-one would know among so many people,
> I only had to slip through the crowd
> To reach out my hand and touch your garment.
>
> It was just a secret touch;
> The touch that changed my life, that made me whole.
> But you knew, Lord.
> You felt my touch, among all those
> Pushing, shoving, jostling people.
>
> It was just a secret touch
> And wonder of wonders, you called me 'Daughter',
> Such a precious moment.
> 'Daughter, your faith has made you whole'
>
> It was just a secret touch.[49]

Maybe much of the ministry of the Reader offers a secret touch. Within the spaces that represent the cell, chapel, chapter, cloister, garden, refectory and scriptorium (and maybe also the infirmary), Readers are ministering and offering a secret touch through their:

> Word-weaving
> Crafting
> Gifts to the distressed[50]

In times of struggle and in times of celebration, for many Readers being ministers of word is a significant part of their calling to licensed lay ministry. It might be said to be their:

> Essence.
> All that makes a thing what it is.
> It's what God calls us to be
> and to give
> in his service[51]

Conclusion

Readers are expressing a sense of vocation to be ministers of word, whether inside church or in the many other areas of life identified by Lings as being lived out in what are potentially sacred spaces. By offering the gifts of the wordsmith together with the desire for all to encounter the Word of God, many lives are being touched through preaching, teaching, formalized pastoral work and incidental conversations. Skilled listening and crafted words offer a 'secret touch' of God in so many ways.

Notes

1 Gloria.
2 M. Leech, 2014, 'Poetry is the Best Theology', *National Catholic Recorder* 25 March 2014, http://ncronline.org/blogs/soul-seeing/poetry-best-theology.
3 A. N. Wilder, 2001, *Theopoetic: Theology and the Religious Imagination*, Lima, OH: Academic Renewal Press.

4 G. Lings, 2009, *Seven Sacred Spaces: Expressing Community Life in Christ*, Encounters on the Edge, no. 43, Sheffield: Church Army. An updated version (2015) is now available, which contains more reflection on how the work is being used and some exercises to apply them. Available by email from ask@churcharmy.org.uk, £4 plus P&P, or from: www.churcharmy.org.uk/Groups/269003/Church_Army/Church_Army/Our_work/Research/Seven_sacred_spaces/Seven_sacred_spaces.aspx.

5 Leo.

6 Leo.

7 Lings, *Seven Sacred Spaces*, p. 6.

8 Leo.

9 Monica.

10 Monica.

11 Monica.

12 Lings, *Seven Sacred Spaces*, p. 10.

13 Monica.

14 Marilyn.

15 John.

16 P. Avis, 1999, *God and the Creative Imagination: Metaphor, Religion and Myth in Religion and Theology*, London: Routledge, p. 11.

17 Avis, *God and the Creative Imagination*, p. 12.

18 Leo.

19 R. Williams, 2014, *The Edge of Words: God and the Habits of Language*, London: Bloomsbury, p. 135.

20 John.

21 Leo.

22 Lings, *Seven Sacred Spaces*, p. 13.

23 Monica.

24 Ruth.

25 The Archbishops' Council, 2000, *Common Worship: Services and Prayers for the Church of England*, London: Church House Publishing, www.churchofengland.org/media/41172/admissionreaders.pdf.

26 Gloria.

27 Gloria.

28 Monica.

29 J. O'Donohue, 2003, *Divine Beauty: The Invisible Embrace*, London: Bantam Books, p. 182.

30 Lings, *Seven Sacred Spaces*, p. 18.

31 Monica.

32 Ruth.

33 www.churchofengland.org/clergy-office-holders/ministry/ministe
   rial-education-and-development/initial-ministerial-education.aspx.
34 Marilyn.
35 Leo.
36 Lings, *Seven Sacred Spaces*, p. 20.
37 Lings, *Seven Sacred Spaces*, p. 21.
38 Ruth.
39 Monica.
40 Marilyn.
41 Lings, *Seven Sacred Spaces*, p. 23.
42 Lings, *Seven Sacred Spaces*, p. 24.
43 Monica.
44 C. D. Pohl, 1999, *Making Room: Recovering Hospitality as a Christian Tradition*, Grand Rapids, MI and Cambridge: Eerdmans, p. 62.
45 Monica.
46 Marilyn.
47 Monica.
48 Gloria.
49 Naomi Smith, March 2014. Unpublished; used with permission.
50 Leo.
51 Gloria.

2

What is a Reader?

PHILLIP TOVEY

This is a question that can be answered in a number of different ways. Some work from a historical perspective; this can be seen in the writing of T. G. King and Rhoda Hiscox.[1] Here the historical approach looks at the development of the ministry and the way it has changed through time. This can be a very useful approach, and Chapter 5 of this book adds another dimension to that history. Others have perhaps a more pragmatic approach in dealing with the implicit theological issues relating to the office in a particular church – Robert Martineau, Cathy Rowling and Paula Gooder, and Gordon Kuhrt and Pat Nappin perhaps come in this category.[2] The discussion of Readers in the context of the doctrine of ministry is perhaps less advanced. Most of the discussion quickly moves from a general view of the laity in the Church to ordained ministries.[3] A few books include a chapter on lay ministries then concentrate more on ordination.[4] Only a few books actually concentrate on lay ministry.[5] There is, however, a series of different types of document that looks at the Church and ministry which, with expansion, may provide a helpful focus for the office of Reader. This includes a variety of church reports, ecumenical agreements and training documents. It is sometimes said that it is not clear what Readers are about, and there lacks a theology of the Reader. To this should be added that there is a continuous discussion about the place of deacon and priest and that the theology of priesthood has yet to be finally agreed. It is clear that there is an ongoing discussion, and that Reader ministry has been developing in a pragmatic way. This could be put in other terms: that it is open to the needs of the Church and the guidance the Spirit.

Baptism, Eucharist and Ministry 1982

The classic ecumenical text *Baptism, Eucharist and Ministry* begins a discussion of ministry with the nature of the Church. Its first section is on 'the calling of the whole people of God', which is its starting point for a discussion of ordained ministry. Within the redemption of the world, the Church exists because of Christ's victory over sin and death. The Church is renewed in the power of the Holy Spirit. It is the work of the Spirit that gives us a starting point to look at Reader ministry.

> The Spirit calls people to faith, sanctifies them through many gifts, gives them strength to witness to the Gospel, and empowers them to serve in hope and love. §3[6]

The two essential aspects of ministry are touched on here: gifting and calling. These concepts will become key in understanding Reader ministry.

Baptism, Eucharist and Ministry goes on to expand the gifting of the Holy Spirit.

> The Holy Spirit bestows on the community diverse and complementary gifts. These are for the common good of the whole people and are manifested in acts of service within the community and the world. They may be gifts of communicating the Gospel in word and deed, gifts of healing, gifts of praying, gifts of teaching and learning, gifts of serving, gifts of guiding and following, gifts of inspiration and vision. §5[7]

In this list, which is not necessarily exhaustive, we can begin to see the place of a Reader.

The document finally goes on to explain some terminology, which will be helpful for us too. Charism 'denotes the gifts bestowed by the Holy Spirit on any member of the body of Christ for the building up of the community and the fulfilment of its calling'. Ministry 'in its broadest sense denotes the service to which the whole people of God is called . . . Ministry or ministries can also denote the particular institutional form which this service may take.' Ordained ministry 'refers to persons who have received a charism and whom the church appoints for service by ordination'.[8] This begins to leave some space for lay ministries and their institutional form. Unfortunately the rest of the document continues to concentrate on ordained ministries and leaves the question of lay ministries hanging.

Lumen Gentium 1964

The movement of thought from the mission of God, to the Church, to ministries, to ordination can also be seen in *Lumen Gentium*, a visionary document from the Second Vatican Council promulgated in 1964.[9] This document begins with a chapter on the mystery of the Church. The starting point is the desire to proclaim the gospel, and this is then spelt out in a Trinitarian way, with design of the Father, the mission of the Son and the sending of the Spirit on the Church. It then examines a number of models of the Church, including a sheepfold, cultivated field, building of God and love. In examining the body of Christ the document states that:

> In that body the life of Christ is communicated to those who believe, and who, through the sacraments, are united in a hidden and real way to Christ in his Passion and glorification. §7

Charism - any good gift which flows from Gods love to human.

Through baptism we are formed in the likeness of Christ and in the Eucharist we have fellowship with Christ and one another. The Spirit is given for the building of the Church:

> according to his own richness and the needs of the ministries, gives his different gifts for the welfare of the Church. §7[10]

It is these gifts that enable the Church to fulfil her mission.

Before a discussion of the hierarchical nature of the Church, an important chapter is included on the people of God. This looks further into the nature of the Church, not least of its being a kingdom of priests:

> The baptized, by regeneration and the anointing of the Holy Spirit, are consecrated to be a spiritual house and a holy priesthood. §10[11]

Through the sacraments the Church is strengthened to perform the task of witness and to spread the faith by word and deed. As the people of God the Church shares in the priestly ministry of Christ and in his prophetic office. The Church's role is to be a living witness to Christ in a life of faith and love and by offering a sacrifice of praise. The Spirit enriches the Church with godly virtues and distributes special graces to 'the faithful of every rank'. By these gifts the Spirit makes them 'fit and ready to undertake various tasks and offices for the renewal and building up of the Church'.[12]

The document contains a wide (fully catholic) vision of the Church, seeing faithful Christians as existing outside of the Roman Catholic Church. It is only after this discussion that the document goes on to talk about the hierarchy of the Church, with the bishop being the successors of the Apostles and the Bishop of Rome being the successor of Peter.

While there are contours in this theology that we may not wish to espouse, the basic direction of the mission of God, the calling of the people of God and their equipping by the Spirit, before any discussion of ordained ministry, is one we can see as ordering our thoughts in a correct way. Too much of the past has started with ordained ministry and then tried to work out an understanding of the laity. This starts with an understanding of the whole Church and then goes on to look at ordained ministry. In this and the previous document the ministry of people God is the starting point, and in that we can then discern lay ministries and ordained ministry.

David Power

An example of developing the theology of the Second Vatican Council can be seen in the work of David Power, *Gifts that Differ: Lay Ministries Established and Unestablished*. He begins by noting the new thinking about minor orders and the permanent diaconate. The minor orders of exorcist and porter were suppressed but those of acolyte and lector were retained, while the notion of a minor 'order' was also suppressed. In reality these two ministries impinge more on ordinands than on parish life in Catholic churches.

David Power invokes two principles with regard to laity and lay ministry. The first comes from the Constitution on Liturgy, which called for 'full and active participation of all the faithful in the church's worship'. He therefore sees these ministries as rooted in the priesthood of the Church and quotes 1 Peter 2.9 'a chosen race, a royal priesthood, a people set apart'. Power goes on to say:

In other words, these ministries are a way of realizing the share in Christ's priestly office which the people receive through the sacraments of initiation.[15]

As such he is expressing a baptismal ecclesiology; ministry rooted in Christ's priesthood as expressed through baptism. Indeed, he says that:

> The theology of ministry, if it is to serve the renewal of its practice, needs to explain how baptism constitutes a call to share in ministry of the church, while at the same time making proper allowance for the sacrament of order.[15]

These are important statements for Anglicans in considering the theology of ministry both for Readers and for the ordained.

David Power sees this theology as rooted in the Second Vatican Council and in the work of Yves Congar. This puts ministry within the context of the faith community, not the other way round. Power's summary of this is:

> It teaches us that the structure of ministry is determined within such a community, on the basis of community need and personal charism, and not merely through the commissioning of single members, by whatever means chosen, whether it be ordination or mandate or blessing. It teaches us that we cannot develop parallel theologies of lay ministry and ordained ministry, but that we have to find a single theology of ministry, within which a theology of the sacrament of order itself may take on a new appearance.[16]

This is an important statement because the danger is that a theology of ordination squeezes out the possibility of lay ministries and of the laity.

How then does David Power distinguish between lay ministries and ordained ministry? He roots this in relationship to the Eucharist.

> Presidency of community and presidency of the eucharist require the charism of leadership . . . Currently theology very

rightly teaches that in the sacrament of order one is simulta-
neously called to the triple ministry of liturgy, preaching and
community presidency.[17]

He sees the order of different ministries as a harmonious one,
found in the common rootedness in baptism. This, however,
seems rather weak in that it locates the charism of leadership as
the fundamental gift of ordained ministry. While it may be true
that leadership is a part of ordained ministry, it is also true that
there are significantly important lay leaders in the Church. The
question would be how all these different forms of leadership
work together; rooted in baptism is his answer. However, the
argument appears to limit leadership to the ordained and as such
needs expanding.

He continues to argue that ordained ministry has a particular
orientation to the Eucharist:

It is the representative nature of the ordained ministry, with
the special relation to eucharistic ministry, that differentiates
it from other ministries.[18]

This does not exclude the possibility of laypeople taking an active
participation in the Eucharist as distributors of the elements.
However, such people are labelled as extra-ordinary ministers
in Catholic language because the relationship is fundamentally
priestly. He does, however, argue that the gifts of the baptized
need to be exercised and discerned. He sees in particular that
many of the baptized have spiritual gifts to interpret God's word
and should be allowed to give the homily at the Eucharist and
other services.

There is much in this theology that is very attractive, and
represents the broad consensus that theologies of ministry
need to be rooted in baptism. They also need to be developed
together, not in separate ways for lay and ordained ministry. Lay

ministry, like ordained ministry, is rooted in baptism, gifts and calling. David Power distinguishes the last two elements in leadership but perhaps a better way would be to ask what type of leadership and how it is orientated to the Eucharist. Reader ministry as a ministry of the Word clearly has an orientation to communion, but of a different nature from that of the priest. *Not sure I understand what this is saying.*

To Equip the Saints 2001

The Berkeley statement of the Sixth International Anglican Liturgical Consultation follows the same theological trajectory as the previous two documents. While the statement is primarily about ordained ministry and rites of ordination, the document begins with the calling of the people of God.

> The whole of creation is called into being through the abundant love of God, who in Christ participates in the world's life so that we may share in the triune life of love and joy. Through the Holy Spirit God baptizes us into the life and ministry of Christ and forms us into the *laos*, the people of God.[19]

The report goes on to stress the importance of baptism.

> The foundation of the life and ministry of the Church is therefore baptism . . . In baptism, the people of God are revealed to be a holy people (1 Peter 2.9–10), ministering to the world in the name and in the manner of Christ.[20]

The document develops by discussing the gifts that are given to the body of Christ to participate in God's mission in the world. It then begins to discuss the relationship between the people of God and the ordained; again it stresses baptism: 'Understanding baptism as the foundation of the life and ministry of the Church (that is, having a baptismal ecclesiology) leads us to see ordained ministers as integral members of the body of Christ.'[21] Along with others, this document stresses the baptismal ministry of the people of God and ministries coming out of this common ecclesiology.

This affirmation of baptismal ecclesiology was questioned by the Inter-Anglican Standing Commission on Ecumenical Relations. The question they posed was: Is baptismal ecclesiology reductionist? It was also questioned by Archbishop Peter Carnley, then Primate of Australia. This perhaps clarifies some of the fear of baptismal ecclesiology, as Archbishop Peter was arguing against the notions of lay presidency put forward from Sydney. In response to this, Louis Weil argues for the foundational nature of baptism, not an ecclesiology that opposes baptism and ordination.[22] It is a question of a Venn diagram, overlapping not opposing circles. Important for lay ministry is the sure foundation of a baptismal ecclesiology for understanding the nature of the Church and its ministries, lay and ordained.

The theology of the Berkeley statement has been included in the ordination rites of the Church of England. At the beginning of the service the bishop introduces the service with a common form for each ordination.

God calls his people to follow Christ, and forms us into a royal priesthood, a holy nation, to declare the wonderful deeds of him who has called us out of darkness into his marvellous light.

The Church is the body of Christ, the people of God and the dwelling place of the Holy Spirit. In baptism the whole Church is summoned to witness to God's love and to work for the coming of his kingdom.[23]

The bishop continues by saying that to serve this royal priesthood a particular office exists and then goes on to explain the office. This puts the people of God and their baptism as prior to ordination. The introduction to *Common Worship: The Admission and Licensing of Readers* unfortunately does not follow the same pathway.

> God has gathered us into the fellowship of the universal Church. As members together of his body, Christ calls us to minister in his name and, according to our gifts, to be instruments of his love in the world. Within this ministry, Readers are called to serve the Church of God and to work together with clergy and other ministers.[24]

Somehow baptismal ecclesiology has faded in this service. However, calling and gifting by the Spirit in the baptismal priesthood gives a clear place for Reader ministry.

Local ministry

The local ministry movement was inspired by the writings of Roland Allen, a missionary to China who contrasted the way mission was conducted by St Paul and was conducted in his day.[25] He pointed out that St Paul travelled in a team in a peripatetic ministry, but appointed local leadership in each of the churches he founded. All who were baptized were expected to minister as part of the body of Christ in service and witness. Allen stressed the importance of the Holy Spirit in equipping local Christians to lead their own churches.

This was then developed in a variety of different places, including New Zealand, the United States and England.[26] There have also been similar discussions in some parts of Roman Catholicism.[27] In England, ministry has been particularly advocated by Andrew Bowden (with a particular concern for the countryside)[28] and by Robin Greenwood. The theological stress is on the gifting by the Spirit of the congregation and an every-member ministry. Often this leads quite quickly to a discussion of ordained ministry and people coming from the congregation for training for priesthood. This has led to a number of ordained local ministry schemes.[29]

Robin Greenwood defines local ministry as:

> the ways in which, increasingly, all Christians, because of their commitment to Christ expressed in baptism, are sharing the ministry that serves God's purposes through the whole church, in many different ways.[30]

He also defines a ministry leadership team consisting of both ordained and licensed ministry and others. He is quite clear that he expects a Reader to be a part of the ministry leadership team.[31] Andrew Bowden and Michael West also expect the Reader to be involved in the ministry team; however, they acknowledge that there may be a threatening situation, particularly when Readers feel that they have committed themselves to substantial theological education and now the team is including people who have not made that sacrifice.[32] Bowden and West continue by showing how a greater consideration of local ministry in one diocese led to a review of Reader ministry, particularly limiting the more sacramental activities of baptism and extended communion.[33] With the possibility of ordained local ministry, the question arises for Readers of the exact nature of their ministry and, if sacramental ministry is desired, why they are not seeking ordination.

The local ministry movement encourages the ministry of all the baptized and its development in lay and ordained ministry as an expression of the local church. Clearly there is a big space for Readers within these ideas, although there has been a move to talk about ordained local ministry and neglect the place of Readers in its concepts. It draws on much of the teaching previously seen, emphasizing a baptismal ecclesiology, the work of the Holy Spirit in giving gifts and the calling of the whole people of God in mission and service.

Edward Hahnenberg

Edward Hahnenberg, a Roman Catholic theologian, develops the notion of baptismal ecclesiology and examines how the different ministries of the Church are united in this approach.[34] Rejecting traditional ontological approaches to ministry, he follows a postmodern trend of looking at ministries as relating to one another. This more organic approach enables him to integrate different ministries in a local church or a diocese in an organic union. As such he brings out the interrelationship seen in the biblical metaphor of the body of Christ.

This he summarizes in a very useful diagram, but one that needs adapting for an Anglican context. Thus I include my version of his diagram adapted to an Anglican ecclesiology (see Figure 2.1).

Figure 2.1 shows a number of different ministries and relates them together in an organic way. It begins with the outside circle, where baptism initiates one into the Church and into general Christian ministry. This at its least, and perhaps most important, is to love your neighbour as yourself. Prayer for and service to the world around and the Church are a part of this general Christian ministry. Then follow a number of occasional Christian ministries. Some of these are regulated and others are

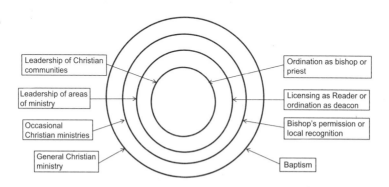

Figure 2.1: Ministries and recognition

not. This would include people who may have permission to preach on occasion or to administer the eucharistic elements. These are often regulated by bishop's licences. But then there are other people who lead house groups and work with children or sing in choirs who have a Christian ministry for a particular occasion.

Hahnenberg distinguishes the next level by having an area of leadership. This will be discerned through gifts and calling. Here I have put the licensing as a Reader or ordination as a deacon, particularly thinking of permanent deacons, of which there are a few in the Church of England. Here the people concerned are set apart for a particular ministry, in the case of Readers, a ministry of the Word, and this is recognized in Canon, liturgy and licensing. There is thus a more public element to the admission of this person than in other ministries. The final area in the chart is that of leadership of communities, which Hahnenberg identifies with bishop and priest. In an Anglican context this needs to be modified with a team element. The bishop works in a senior leadership team including archdeacons and deans, and is responsible to the diocesan synod. A priest works in a ministry team, with other priests, deacons and Readers, and works in conjunction with the church council.

Further Anglican thinking

A number of Anglican writers have tried to develop a theology of ministry both lay and ordained. An older work was that by Robert Martineau, *The Office and Work of a Reader*.[35] He starts by saying that one of the principal reasons for the revival of the office was 'to enable the laity to have a due share in the ministry of the Word'.[36] His reasoning after that is somewhat pragmatic but he sees the Reader as the local minister as distinct from the more itinerant priest, and makes a strong point that Readers are admitted to a lifelong office, therefore when they move they may be relicensed but are not readmitted.

Steven Croft, in *Ministry in Three Dimensions*, is primarily interested in ordained ministry.[37] He is aware of the development of lay ministries and sees baptism as the foundation of the ministry of the people of God. The calling of all the baptized is to participate in the mission and ministry of God. In looking at the ministry of the Church he sees this centred in ordained ministry, but alongside that he has what he calls charismatic ministries. This is only partially touched on in his work, and it appears he is thinking of Early Church prophets more than current lay ministries. However, his model could be modified to include them, as in Figure 2.2.

The modifications made in Figure 2.2 are to use the English terms for the threefold order but also to rethink the charismatic ministries. Croft talks about charismatic ministries, meaning, for example, prophet. But there are other ministries, based on gift and charism, that were soon recognized, such as the office of Reader.

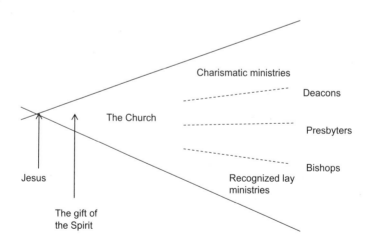

Figure 2.2: Croft's model modified

Bridging the Gap: Reader Ministry Today is a collection of essays trying to answer the question: What is a Reader?[38] This perhaps is an unfortunate starting point as it does what David Power warned against, starting with a ministry rather than the whole ministry of the people of God. It suggests that Readers are a bridge between the laity and clergy, and this is the fundamental model of the book. The argument that the Reader has one foot in the world and one foot in the Church is undermined by self-supporting ministers (or worker priests) who find themselves in a similar context. Context alone is an insufficient basis for developing a theology of lay ministry.

For Such a Time as This was the 2001 House of Bishops report on the renewal of the diaconate. Its writers were aware that it needed to deal with lay ministry and knew of other reports that began with the calling of the whole people of God. However, the report rather quickly moves from that fundamental position to concentrating on the diaconate. In picking up the work of John Collins on the deacon, it tends to distinguish between discipleship in the ministry of all the people of God and the ministry that has a representative role. The report is clear that there are ministries that are lay ministries, mentioning Readers and churchwardens; however, historically in this category should be considered deaconesses, evangelists and authorized lay ministers. Also rarely discussed in Anglican documents is the position of those in religious orders.

While being positive about Readers the report struggles to make a distinction that is clear without sounding negative.

Readers belong within the representative (publicly acknowledge and accountable) ministry of the Church. Yet their ministry remains a lay one. Reader ministry is an office rather than an order . . . the office of Reader is not an 'ecclesial sign' in the same way that the ordained ministry is. It is not irrevocable like the orders of deacons, priests and bishops.[39]

44

There is a sense in which the report would seem to prefer to have a renewed order of deacons that leads to the withering away of Reader ministry. This, however, is not the ecclesial reality, with continuing numbers of people coming forward for Reader ministry but very few for the permanent diaconate.

In 2008 the Church of England produced a major report on Readers, *Reader Upbeat*. This is a large complex report with 30 different recommendations, each diocese being asked to respond to these recommendations in their own ways. It had conducted a survey of Reader ministry and has an extensive historical investigation of the development of Reader ministry. Much shorter is the section of the theology of Reader ministry, which covers two pages.

Unlike the theologies we have so far considered, *Reader Upbeat* confines itself to a consideration of the meaning of the word 'ministry'.[40] It particularly becomes entangled in the work of John Collins, who has written extensively in this area. He argued that *diakonia* in the New Testament doesn't mean general service, in the sense of humble work, but is a commissioned service, more like an ambassador.[41] He has argued strongly in terms of the diaconal ministry, supporting the development of the diaconate of the Second Vatican Council.[42] He has, however, argued against the development of lay ecclesial ministries and against the ecclesiology espoused by Hahnenberg.[43] Collins therefore wanted to argue that lay ministers should be ordained deacon. He also argues that there is no general ministry of the baptized. While his views have been generally accepted on the meaning of the word *diakonia*, there are people who question the practical implications he draws out from his position. Paul Avis gives a stronger view for the ministry of the baptismal priesthood.[44] Paula Gooder suggests that commissioned service can include lay ministries such as churchwarden and Reader.[45] *Reader Upbeat* seems to argue for a modified position. It is uncomfortable with every-member ministry because it views this as diluting the definition of ministry,

[handwritten note: diakonia 'the specific kind to help any people in need. Some times refers to Service among others.]

but it also criticizes Collins for tightening too much his definitions and suggests that commissioned service can be outside of ordained ministry. It could have been a lot stronger in this last comment, following the work of Paula Gooder, and it could have argued the antiquity of the office of Reader, contra Collins' strong insistence on the diaconate. Readers today are people commissioned for a task in the Church.

It is unfortunate that this report was so lightweight in this particular area. It is aware of a baptismal ecclesiology but does not seem to grasp its implications at all. As such it omits to discuss a theology that might well support Reader ministry more clearly.

John Collins

We have touched above on the work of John Collins, who is undoubtedly an important voice in this discussion. As can be seen, he is increasingly influencing Anglican thinking, particularly on the diaconate, which raises the question of how that order links to other ministries. His original work was to look at the meaning of *diakonia* and has fairly conclusively argued that this does not mean lowly or menial service but a commission from God to do a particular task (mostly teaching or evangelization or both).[46] There are, however, quite a number of questions about the implications he draws out in other writings.

In a follow-up work he argues against the notion of every-member ministry, which he seems to interpret in a way that is antithetical; that is, either every-member ministry or an ordained ministry.[47] He reinterprets the passages on spiritual gifts, particularly in 1 Corinthians 12 and in Ephesians, successfully pointing to the change in interpretation of these passages from his work on *diakonia*. In the 1 Corinthians passage he distinguishes between two types of gifts, ministry and 'energies'. This is dependent on the meaning of *diakonia* in the passage, which he argues refers to commissioned ministers whose role is in teaching and prophesying; a ministry of the word of God.[48] This, however, does not exclude the 'energies', which are types of charismatic gift scattered through the Church, although he does not discuss this aspect of Paul's writing. Nor does he comment on the fact that prophecy is mentioned in the discussion of energies, where his interpretation seems to suggest it is a *diakonia*. In Ephesians he points out the significant change in the translation, which refocuses ministry from the ordained to the whole Church. While this is clearly a rethinking of the interpretation of the passage, questions of *diakonia* are not explicitly referenced in the text and there is no reason why one cannot have commissioned ministers and an every-member ministry. Later he seems to imply that the growth of laypeople ministering in the Church is a bad development within Roman Catholicism, and what is needed is a flourishing of the orders of deacon and priest.[49]

How this translates into Anglicanism is something of concern. While it may change our view of some scriptural texts, Anglicanism has clearly kept a 'hierarchy' and distinguishes between gifts of the whole people of God and particular people who are called ministry. In one way *diakonia* as commissioned ministry, with a connection to teaching and the Word, is exactly the ministry of Readers. This ministry is ancient and grew alongside a transforming office of deacon. Collins' argument might suggest some fruitfulness in the notion of 'minor orders'. Having been suppressed at the Reformation they were revived in the Church of England in the 1860s with the development of deaconesses, evangelists, lay workers and Readers, this building on experience of lay workers in overseas mission, bringing it into home mission. All of these 'minor orders' are various forms of commissioned ministry with various tasks for the building of God's kingdom. Collins' work is important but the application of it to the Anglican context is an ongoing issue.

47

The Mission and Ministry of the Whole Church 2007

This report was a follow-up to *For Such a Time as This*, which had been deemed not to have done the work required in a thorough enough way.[50] *The Mission and Ministry of the Whole Church* is a more substantial report, and while looking at the diaconate, investigates other lay ministries in depth. It also begins with Collins' work but considers *diakonia* in light of other ministries, including churchwarden, lay pastoral assistant, Church Army and Reader.

A very helpful section identifies the issue of overlap in ministry. It points out that there is always such an overlap; through his body the Church, Christ ministers as prophet, priest and king to a needy world. Thus the whole Church in some way participates in the ministry of Christ. However, there are those who are called and commissioned to minister who exercise *diakonia*. The report particularly looks to three areas of ministry: preaching and teaching; assisting with the sacraments; pastoral care. Different ministries have different mixes of these areas. In many of the ministries there is an overlap with a different distinct ministry. So distinctiveness is not because of unique function but because of the calling and commission. Thus the report rightly says that while Readers and deacons have very similar functions, there are fundamental differences in the call and commission. As such it points out the weakness of a purely functional view of ministry.

The report has very positive things to say about Readers. It points out that within the Church this is a large and active lay ministry, which has varied in its functions through time. The present version in the Church of England is one of a ministry of the Word. Like *Reader Upbeat*, it does not look to a growing sacramental role for Readers, pointing out that like anyone they can baptize in emergency, and with the bishop's permission lead services of communion by extension. Rather it looks to the possible missional opportunities of this lay ministry.

As a lay ministry it is an office rather than an order, and this is shown in the way the ministry begins not by the laying on of hands, as clergy are ordained, but with an admission to an office. This distinction is an ancient one, indicating a difference between a holy order and an office.[51]

In considering the significant overlap between Readers and deacons, it hopes that many Readers will want to be ordained deacon and that the two might work together. While a number of Readers do later seek ordination, there are very few who wish to become deacons, the vast majority looking to priesthood. So this aspect of the report seemed to be unconvincing. Rather it could have developed further the application of *diakonia* to Reader ministry and the implications of that.

Towards a model of Reader ministry

This chapter has tried to survey a wide range of opinions of ministry, lay and ordained. Part of the issue is to find a way to discuss the theology of Readers as a part of the ministry of the Church. There is a broad ecumenical consensus about certain parameters for understanding the Church and ministry, with a lone voice in Paul Collins arguing in a different direction. This chapter has taken his work into consideration and will pick up some of the major conclusions that are derived from his early work, while not being convinced by some of the ways he decides to apply that research to the present context. The conclusions significantly take into account Collins' work and then apply them to Readers.

There are two key aspects of the ecumenical consensus that need to be considered first. One is that the theological approach to ministry should start with the whole Church first and then look at particular ministers. Thus one should start with the priesthood of the Church and look then at the nature of priest-hood in its ministers, not the other way round. One of Collins' weaknesses is that he has not done this with deacons and *dia-konia*. The other aspect is that a theology of ministry, lay and ordained, needs to be developed together even if in the end one is going to concentrate on a particular ministry. Both Hahnenberg and Croft have developed useful diagrams to explain their view. The diagram in Figure 2.3 is offered as a model to include ministries lay and ordained. It is an attempt to do this through Anglican eyes and in particular through someone in the Church of England.

Figure 2.3 begins with the baptismal priesthood of believers (the large ellipse), which is the Church of all the faithful. It picks up the ecumenical consensus, as well as the work done by Anglican liturgists, that the starting point to understand ministry is the call of the whole Church to follow Christ, and the equipping

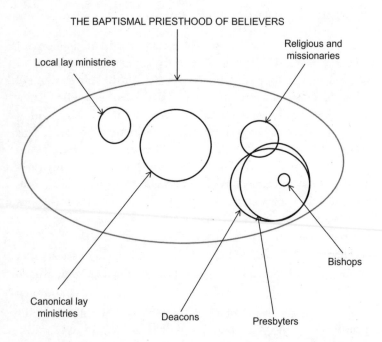

Figure 2.3: A ministry model

of the Church by the Holy Spirit. This does not by definition make each individual Christian a minister but it does mean that each Christian will have some sort of ministry according to the gifts they are given. As one continues in discipleship then new gifts may be given and a new calling may be heard.

It is helpful next to look at the five circles and one smaller ellipse. These are all forms of commissioned ministry of different sorts but ultimately have a call from Christ to a particular task.

The first circle to look at is canonical lay ministries. These are those recognized by the Church of England by canon. This category includes Readers, lay workers and evangelists/Church Army. These are all admitted to office in diverse ways, but once admitted may have times of abeyance but will only be relicensed after a renewed call. These are laypeople exercising *diakonia* called by Christ and recognized by the national Church.

The second circle to look at is lay commissioned ministries. These may be recognized at a diocesan level, for example where dioceses have lay pastoral ministers, authorized preachers or funeral ministers. They may also be recognized by parishes, where parishes may employ administrators, youth workers, pastoral ministers and children's workers. These people may have considerable expertise in particular areas and their role is recognized by a diocese or parish. These are laypeople exercising *diakonia* called by Christ and with church recognition and commission. There may be in this category some people with a canonical recognition, for example churchwardens, sidespeople and parish clerks, but this canonical recognition is not to a lifelong office.

The third circle to look at is religious and missionaries. Here people are commissioned to particular callings by the religious society or mission society for tasks here and overseas. Increasingly these two types of societies are coming together as they recognize common patterns in each other. These are not canonically recognized ministries because the Church has yet to catch up canonically with the existence of these groups. Clearly in both there may be laypeople as well as deacons and priests. These also exercise *diakonia*, having particular callings to outreach and lives of prayer.

The smaller ellipse represents the office of deacon. It is deliberately drawn elliptical to enable the possibility of a permanent diaconate. Indeed, while this chapter has not centred on discussions of the diaconate, I believe there is an important place for a permanent diaconate to exist within the Church. In the Church of England this is always obscured by the transitional diaconate, and in recent years this has been more complicated by the discussion of the ordination of women. The diaconate is a called and commissioned group to minister God's Word to his people and world. Here too *diakonia* is exercised in the Church and society.

The circle labelled 'presbyters' does not completely overlap with that of deacons because the possibility of direct ordination to the presbyterate is envisaged. This will be discussed later. Here priesthood is exercised. Finally, the circle labelled 'bishops' is where *episcope* is exercised, primarily by the bishops of the Church but as Stephen Croft points out, such oversight is often delegated to presbyters. In his concentration on *diakonia* Collins has not discussed the nature of the other two dimensions of ministry, priesthood and *episcope*, and so needs to be supplemented by the work of, for example, Stephen Croft.[52]

In this entire diagram leadership can be exercised by anyone equipped by God to do so and gifts of leadership are seen to be possible in all the sets. Laypeople, for example, may have key roles of leadership in projects that they develop, such as stewardship, or in the structures of church, such as in leadership in the house of laity.

It is usual to argue that presbyters and bishops must first be ordained deacon in order that they may be servants of the Church. This particular argument has three problems. It does not sufficiently deal with the history of ordination by steps, the *cursus honorum*, which shows that this is not an absolute in the history of the Church.[53] Second, it can sound somewhat insulting ecumenically where Methodists and Lutherans, for example, are directly ordained to the presbyterate, and they seem to have no more problems than the rest of us with presbyters lacking a certain humility. Third, it has not really taken on board the implications of Paul Collins and *diakonia* in relationship to lay ministries. This is particularly pertinent to Readers who wish to get ordained. In the model above they have been exercising a ministry of *diakonia* maybe for a number of years. If their calling develops into sacramental ministry as well as a ministry of the Word, then because of their previous exercise of *diakonia* there is a strong argument for direct ordination to the presbyterate. They will already be recognized by their congregations as ministers of the gospel; their ministry is now changing into a presbyteral form.

Thus the ministry of Reader is a call and commissioned ministry recognized by the Church. It is an office of ancient beginnings and has grown and developed as it responds to the call of God and the needs of ministry. It is an office that exercises *diakonia*. People who are called to such an office give order to the baptismal priesthood in a ministry of the Word.

Conclusions

The work of John Collins is of importance not only in the discussion of the diaconate but also in other lay ministries. As yet it has only been initially considered in relationship to Reader ministry. This chapter is a contribution towards that growing understanding. Reader ministry is rooted in the baptismal priesthood and is discerned by the Church through an examination of gifts and calling. It then begins by a service of admission that is lifelong with an ongoing oversight by licence. It has ancient roots but continues to be flexible according to its shaping by the Spirit for the mission of God. It was called by T. G. King 'a pioneer ministry'. The future probably points to an ongoing pioneer role in the mission of the Church.

Notes

1 T. G. King, 1973, *Readers: A Pioneer Ministry*, London: Myland Fund; R. Hiscox, 1988, 'The Development of Reader Ministry', *Modern Churchman* 30, pp. 31–7; R. Hiscox, 1991, *Celebrating Reader Ministry*, London: Mowbray.

2 R. Martineau, 1980, *The Office and Work of a Reader*, London: Mowbray; G. W. Kuhrt and P. Nappin, 2002, *Bridging the Gap: Reader Ministry Today*, London: Church House Publishing; C. Rowling and P. Gooder, 2009, *Reader Ministry Explored*, London: SPCK.

3 S. J. L. Croft, 1999, *Ministry in Three Dimensions: Ordination and Leadership in the Local Church*, London: Darton, Longman & Todd.

4 S. K. Wood, 2000, *Sacramental Orders*, Collegeville, MN: Liturgical Press.

5 D. N. Power, 1980, *Gifts that Differ: Lay Ministries Established and Unestablished*, New York: Pueblo.

6 World Council of Churches, 1982, *Baptism, Eucharist and Ministry*, Geneva: World Council of Churches, p. 20.

7 World Council of Churches, *Baptism, Eucharist and Ministry*, p. 20.

8 World Council of Churches, 1982, *Baptism, Eucharist and Ministry*, p. 21.

9 A. Flannery, 1992, *Vatican Council II: The Conciliar and Post-Conciliar Documents*, Leominster: Fowler Wright, pp. 350–426.

10 Flannery, *Vatican Council II*, p. 355.

11 Flannery, *Vatican Council II*, pp. 360–1.

12 Flannery, *Vatican Council II*, p. 363.

13 Power, *Gifts that Differ*.

14 Power, *Gifts that Differ*, p. 8.

15 Power, *Gifts that Differ*, p. 133.

16 Power, *Gifts that Differ*, p. 61.

17 Power, *Gifts that Differ*, p. 139.

18 Power, *Gifts that Differ*, p. 162.

19 P. Gibson, 2002, *Anglican Ordination Rites – The Berkeley Statement: To Equip the Saints: Findings of the Sixth International Anglican Liturgical Consultation, Berkeley, California, 2001*, Cambridge: Grove Books, p. 4.

20 Gibson, *Anglican Ordination Rites*, p. 4.

21 Gibson, *Anglican Ordination Rites*, p. 5.

22 L. Weil, 2006, 'Baptismal Ecclesiology: Uncovering a Paradigm' in R. L. Dowling and D. Holeton, *Equipping the Saints: Ordination in Anglicanism Today: Papers from the Sixth International Anglican Liturgical Consultation*, Blackrock, Co. Dublin, Columba Press, pp. 18–34.

23 Church of England, 2007, *Common Worship: Ordination Services*, London: Church House Publishing, p. 10.

24 Church of England, 2007, *Common Worship: The Admission and Licensing of Readers*, London: Archbishops' Council, www.churchofengland.org/media/41172/admissionreaders.pdf, p. 5.

25 R. Allen, 1912, 1962, *Missionary Methods: St. Paul's or ours?*, Grand Rapids, MI: Eerdmans.

26 J. Borgeson and L. Wilson, 1990, *Reshaping Ministry: Essays in Memory of Wesley Frensdorff*, Arvada, CO. Jethro Publications; B. Hartless, 2009, *Sharing Local Ministry*, Blandford Forum: Parish and People.

27 F. Lobinger, 1999, *Like his Brothers and Sisters: Ordaining Community Leaders*, New York: Crossroad.

28 A. Bowden, 1994, *Ministry in the Countryside: A Model for the Future*, London and New York: Mowbray.

29 Advisory Board of Ministry, 1998, *Stranger in the Wings*, London: Church House; M. Torry and J. Heskins, 2006, *Ordained Local Ministry: A New Shape for Ministry in the Church of England*, London: Canterbury Press.

30 R. Greenwood, 2000, *The Ministry Team Handbook*, London: SPCK, p. xi.

31 Greenwood, *Ministry Team Handbook*, p. 20.

32 A. Bowden and M. West, 2000, *Dynamic Local Ministry*, London and New York: Continuum, p. 62.

33 Bowden and West, 2000, *Dynamic Local Ministry*, p. 162.

34 E. P. Hahnenberg, 2003, *Ministries: A Relational Approach*, New York: Crossroad.

35 Martineau, *Office and Work of a Reader*.

36 Martineau, *Office and Work of a Reader*, p. 1.

37 Croft, *Ministry in Three Dimensions*.

38 Kuhrt and Nappin, *Bridging the Gap*.

39 House of Bishops Working Party, 2001, *For Such a Time as This: A Renewed Diaconate in the Church of England: A Report to the General Synod of the Church of England of a Working Party of the House of Bishops*, London: Church House Publishing, p. 41.

40 Reader Review Group, 2008, *Reader Upbeat: Quickening the Tempo of Reader Ministry in the Church Today: A Report*, London: General Synod of the Church of England, pp. 23–4.

41 J. N. Collins, 1990, *Diakonia: Re-interpreting the Ancient Sources*, New York: Oxford University Press.

42 J. N. Collins, 2002, *Deacons and the Church: Making Connections Between Old and New*, Leominster: Gracewing; Harrisburg, PA: Morehouse.

43 J. N. Collins, 2005a, 'Fitting Lay Ministries into a Theology of Ministry', *Worship* 79, pp. 209–22; J. N. Collins, 2005b, 'Fitting Lay Ministries into a Theology of Ministry: Responding to an American Consensus', *Worship* 79, pp. 152–67.

44 P. D. L. Avis, 2005, *A Ministry Shaped by Mission*, London: T. & T. Clark.

45 P. Gooder, 2006, '*Diakonia* in the New Testament: A Dialogue with John N. Collins', *Ecclesiology* 3, pp. 33–56.

46 J. N. Collins, 1990, *Diakonia: Re-interpreting the Ancient Sources*, New York: Oxford University Press.

47 J. N. Collins, 1992, *Are all Christians ministers?*, Collegeville, MN: Liturgical Press.

48 J. N. Collins, 1993, 'Ministry as a Distinct Category among the Charismata (1 Corinthians 12:4–7)', *Neotestamentic* 27, pp. 79–91.

49 Collins, 2005b, 'Fitting Lay Ministries into a Theology of Ministry: Responding to an American Consensus', pp. 152–67; Collins, 2005a, 'Fitting Lay Ministries into a Theology of Ministry', pp. 209–22.

50 Faith and Order Advisory Group, 2007, *The Mission and Ministry of the Whole Church: Biblical, Theological and Contemporary Perspectives*, London: General Synod of the Church of England.

51 See P. F. Bradshaw, 2013, *Rites of Ordination: Their History and Theology*, Collegeville, MN: Liturgical Press, pp. 47–9.

52 Croft, *Ministry in Three Dimensions*.

53 J. S. H. Gibaut, 2000, *The Cursus Honorum: A Study of the Origins and Evolution of Sequential Ordination*, New York: P. Lang.

3

Ministry in the World

SALLY BUCK

Readers are often identified by their blue scarves. This may lead to the assumption that a Reader is only exercising ministry when robed and taking part in acts of liturgy. As noted in Chapter 1, on Reader ministry as a ministry of word, there are many places and expressions of ministry that do not depend on the liturgical or even church-based role for a person to consider what they are doing to be an outworking of their Reader training and to be incorporated in their admission and licensing to the role. Encouraged to seek to understand the world, the Church's mission and ministry in the world and to communicate the gospel both inside and outside of church, Readers are expected to see their role as extending beyond this traditional, blue-scarves, liturgical role. It is the intention of this chapter to give voice to a number of Readers whose main expression of their ministry falls outside the traditional role. Their stories are told in their own words to enable them to communicate the passion they feel for the world in which they minister. All seek to point others to God, Father, Son and Holy Spirit. These people's expressions of ministry are representative of many others whose main expressions of ministry are world- rather than church-facing. This chapter celebrates these, and by association, other ministries.

Three of those who share with us are involved in chaplaincies of one sort or another. These are maybe more commonly experienced expressions of ministry (both lay and ordained). Others, though, tell of their sense of vocation being expressed in their places of employment or in their involvement in their local communities. While the individual patterns of ministry are different, perhaps there is one image that ties all of them together. Ministry more broadly is often described in terms of walking alongside others. Most frequently that walking is spoken of metaphorically. On occasions, though, the physical act of walking alongside others is a way of creating space and a mutual focus and aim. Within this space it is possible to have conversations, to challenge, to laugh and to cry in a way that face-to-face meetings often do not, and sermons and group meetings could not, allow for.

> While they were talking and discussing, Jesus himself came near and went with them, but their eyes were kept from recognizing him. . . . When he was at the table with them, he took bread, blessed and broke it, and gave it to them. Then their eyes were opened, and they recognized him. (Luke 24.15–16, 30–31 NRSV)

My own experience of walking alongside others in a physical way belongs to the years that our family spent as part of the community of Scargill House, a retreat house and conference centre in the Yorkshire Dales. Much of our ministry was spent walking with guests. Conversations often covered topics of depth and humour, sadness and joy, in the space of a few hundred yards.

Jesus walked alongside the disciples on their way back to Emmaus. They seem to have felt dejected and alone, their plans all having come to nothing and life returning to the mundane and the normal after their time following Jesus and expecting such great things of him. Their immediate response to Jesus was less than enthusiastic. He was not recognized until he performed the familiar act of breaking bread and sharing food with them. In a similar way, ministry that involves physically or metaphorically walking alongside others is offered by people who long to bring the reality of Christ's love into often difficult situations.

The stories that are offered throughout this chapter are shared by those whose ministry as Readers involves them in walking alongside people, sometimes in difficult circumstances and sometimes in the mundane and ordinary times of their lives. Many Readers are spending the majority of their ministry with people who feel sidelined, alone and misunderstood. Those who share with us here are called by God to minister in places that are often unseen. I want to thank them for sharing their very personal stories with us and to encourage others to tell their stories of God's calling and enabling in ministry.

Quality Assurance (QA) in Education

Before any of us can offer ourselves in ministry, whatever that ministry might look like, we will have taken part in a process of discernment, selection and training. This process is moderated and held to account by a group of people tasked with ensuring its quality. Thanks to those who offer their gifts and skills in this way, the quality of training of Readers is going from strength to strength. David Hanson was licensed as a reader in Southwark Diocese in 2011. He works in the Church of England's Ministry Division as quality assurance administrator for ministerial training, and in that role supports the teams that review and report on the Church's ministerial training colleges and courses. Reviewers might be ministers, theologians, university or schoolteachers, or business and resource managers; and all will have local church commitments. David's role involves briefing reviewers and staff colleagues and coordinating people, paperwork and timetables.

When asked to consider how this role relates to his Reader ministry, David's initial response was 'I hadn't really thought about it quite like that, but I guess in quite a few ways it does. It's about quality, after all.' While this work draws on David's professional skills of management and administration, he sees it as being part of a whole and that 'work done and gifts offered in God's service need to be the best they can be. That's true for ministerial training, and for individual ministries.'

David goes on to reflect on his role by saying:

> It's about recognizing and honouring great teaching and staff in training colleges and courses. St Paul often signs off by remembering by name his fellow-workers and what they mean to him. Readers sometimes say that kind of value and respect for people's input could play a bigger part in the Church's life. The same goes for QA. Does the assessment framework leave enough room to commend achievement? Does it help colleagues to share good practice? With the Church's main partner university, Durham, we're working on that.

David's role embodies the need to learn from others, and from the example of Jesus who 'constantly challenges those who think they are wise to be open to new perspectives'. Ministry often leads to questions – difficult ones sometimes, says David. He goes on to say that the questions are not the problem, but that:

> It's when the feedback stops that you've really got a problem. And in developing QA, Ministry Division is a learner too. Reviewers and training colleagues want a streamlined, quicker process and clearer, up-to-date outcomes and are offering ideas about how to do it. Again, work in progress.

> For me it's about personal awareness and development, as with any job and any ministry. I get to brief reviewers far more expert in training and ministry than I am about how QA works. It can sometimes feel a bit like preaching to people who have life experiences and knowledge that you haven't. Theological knowledge too, which can be scary. We've all been

there; and pretending to be wise never works. The only answer is to be committed and genuine about your own message.

It's about the value of every role: learners and disciples; teachers, leaders and ministers; even quality assurance staff. Every participant is essential to the Church's life, St Paul says. Whether QA administration counts as a more or less honourable part of the body of Christ, others can judge. Generally they do so with kindness and courtesy: a true mark of Christian charity.

Most of all, it's about enthusiasm for excellence and for service. Training colleagues demonstrate that. And so do reviewers, who bring to this role their time and expertise, and their commitment to the Church's flourishing and to training that will best equip ministers, ordained and lay, to reach out and share the gospel with God's people. It's a joy to work with them and, often, a reminder of what ministry – licensed and otherwise – is about.

In all that David speaks of, the desire to be an encourager of others and to have an expectation of quality that honours God and respects those among whom he works is evident.

A Scientist

Someone else who speaks of his ministry in terms of questioning and aiming to find quality responses to the questions of faith that impact on our society in the twenty-first century is Chris Knight. Chris's work involves him in giving talks in a university setting on the relationship between science and Christianity. He says that 'Responding to students' questions gives a fascinating insight into the sorts of questions that they have, as well as revealing their more general attitudes to Christianity – often sympathetic but occasionally hostile.'

Quoting Blaise Pascal, who claimed that '[people] despise religion . . . The cure for this is first to show that religion is not contrary to reason, but worthy of reverence and respect. Next make it attractive, make good [people] wish it were true, and then show that it is',[1] Chris reflects on his own experience of questioning faith but wishing that he could believe as a teenager. He says that his journey properly began when he found good reasons to believe.

Chris's reflection explores the fact that he found that 'faith did not need to be blind'. He develops this thinking by saying:

Indeed, it *should* not be blind: because we are told to love God with our *minds* (Mark 12.30) and always to be ready to *defend* our beliefs before anyone who asks us the reason for our hope in Christ (1 Peter 3.15). As a scientist, I needed reason and evidence to be a firm foundation for what I believed – and eventually found that that seemed to be God's perspective as well. It is the middle stage of Gerard Hughes' three stages of growth in belief: infancy, adolescence and adulthood (see Chapter 2 of his *God of Surprises*). Neglecting any stage results in imbalance, but neglecting the adolescent questioning (and answers) results in belief that 'comes to be considered a private but harmless eccentricity of a minority'[2] – an apt description of how many people view Christians today.

On ending a 22-year career in scientific research, I explored what my future should look like. With the success of Dan Brown's *The Da Vinci Code* and the rise of the New Atheists following Richard Dawkins' book *The God Delusion*, I was asked to provide responses to their claims for my church congregation. This 'defence' of Christian beliefs has the rather technical term of 'apologetics'. Since apologetics was instrumental in bringing me to faith (or at least in removing the barriers that prevented me from a proper consideration of it), I had continued to have an interest in answering people's questions. I realized the importance of responding to the challenges Dan Brown, Richard Dawkins and others presented – to Christians and non-Christians alike. I recognized God's call to a greater involvement in this wider area   and this led to training as a Reader and working on an apologetics website (www.bethinking.org) that aims to prepare students to communicate and defend their Christian beliefs at university and beyond. The website is used by many non-students as well!

Considering again Pascal's statement quoted earlier, Christian involvement in projects like food banks, anti-trafficking campaigns and Street Pastors can often make people *wish* Christianity to be true. They *want* to believe, but have barriers to faith or simply see no reason to believe. For many these barriers are rational and, as Christians, we often feel ill-equipped to help people see that Christianity is both reasonable and true. I see this as a part of what all Christians are called to do (1 Peter 3.15 again) – and a part of what Readers should particularly be prepared to do and model. One of the questions asked by the bishop in the Readers' Licensing Service is: 'Will you be diligent in prayer, in reading Holy Scripture, and in all studies that will deepen your faith and fit you to bear witness to the truth of the gospel?' We respond 'By the grace of God, I will.'[3] A significant part of my Christian ministry is attempting 'to bear witness to the truth of the gospel' and providing resources to enable others to do the same. But I believe that this defence and commendation of our beliefs is an important aspect of the ministries of all Readers, commending our faith to others in a reasonable manner, encouraging them to love God with their mind, and sustaining them in times of doubt.

Chris's expression of his ministry is congruent with both his personality and his own experience of faith. He is a teacher of the faith in a very specific way, one that gives him a voice as a layperson in a world that touches the lives of many people who would not enter a church as the first port of call when struggling with questions of faith. Readers have historically been given the role of catechist. As those who teach the principles of Christian religion, usually to those already involved in a church community, catechists are maybe the original apologists. Chris's expression of his Reader ministry builds on, and develops, that proven role.

A Coach and Consultant

The teaching aspect of Reader ministry is developed further by Andy Smith. Licensed as a Reader in Leicester Diocese in 2013, Andy works as a coach and consultant supporting 'individuals on personal development and individuals and teams on achieving business goals'. His ministry and his work are intertwined in a way that emphasizes the lay nature of his calling. Reflecting on his interpretation of his ministry, Andy asks whether Reader ministry is a ministry of the Word or of the ear. He writes:

I consider myself fortunate to have begun my ministry as a Reader in 2013 at about the same time I started working as a business coach and consultant. As I look back after two and a half years I'm astonished to see how closely these two elements of my life overlap. I become aware of an increasing sense that my roles as a Reader and as a business coach are more closely entwined than I realized.

My progression through selection, training, licensing and now ministry as a Reader has led me to an ever increasing sense of purpose, to 'grow disciples', to work with those already in a relationship with God. It doesn't matter if the relationship is a new or long-standing one, we all need to continually grow and deepen our discipleship and my call is to support people in achieving this.

At the same time, my business is rooted in a deep-seated belief that every single person on earth is capable of the most extraordinary things – but that most people may need some help and support to think through what this means for them, and how to achieve it. This is the role of the coach, and sees me working with individuals on personal development and with individuals and teams on achieving business goals.

Reflecting on the past two and a half years, I see an increasing harmony of purpose and skills needed to do both these things effectively. Sir John Whitmore (a leading business coach) says that 'Coaching is unlocking people's potential to maximize their own performance. It is helping them to learn rather than teaching them.'[4] I do this in my work as business coach and Reader, and while most of my business clients may not (currently) consider themselves to 'have a faith', nonetheless they are all part of God's creation. In helping them fulfil their potential I believe that I too am playing a small part in God's plan. After all, doesn't Paul write in Ephesians 2.10, 'For we are all God's workmanship, created in Christ Jesus to do good works'? And in the process of getting to know my clients really well, there are inevitably many occasions when my ministry and faith crop up in conversation anyway. Nothing heavy, but from little seeds . . .

Andy goes on to consider the skills of the coach to quickly gain the trust of the client through listening intently to their context and needs. He explains that:

every person's story is unique, and the effective coach listens to that story before attempting to engage with it, while understanding that every client, whether 'of faith' or not, seeks to be understood and to grow emotionally, professionally, spiritually and socially. Active listening develops trust between coach and client, which leads to greater insight and in turn to greater results.

This reflection on his work context leads Andy to reconsider the importance of listening in his Reader ministry, recognizing that 'In growing disciples as a Reader I also need to listen before then encouraging, challenging and teaching my fellow disciples, and in doing so serve them.' He refers to the Dutch priest and writer Henri Nouwen, who says that 'Listening is a form of spiritual hospitality by which you invite strangers to become friends, to get to know their inner selves more fully, and even to dare to be silent with you.'[5]

Andy wonders: 'Is that a good thought for all of us who preach, teach and lead worship to bear in mind as we celebrate and build on 150 years of Reader ministry?'

Allotment ministry

Someone who spends much of her time in silence, whether alone or with others, is Karin Silk. Karin was licensed as a Reader in 1993 to the Diocese of Lincoln and serves Jesus in the parish of Swallowbeck alongside her husband Ian, who is the parish priest. Karin relates the story of an allotment that has become a place of ministry – of being alongside people and a place where food can be grown and shared. She says that the allotment, when she first took it on, was set in a corner by a footpath lined with trees, behind some sheltered-housing flats and next to a play park and fields. The allotment was not consciously taken on as a place where Karin could exercise ministry. She reflects on the fact that:

Initially, I liked the quietness of this place to go to for a break from the demands of life at the vicarage and in some ways it proved to be just that – no roads, no expectations, wild flowers in the un-taken plots and birds nearby, fresh air and the scents of earth and growing vegetation. I wouldn't have said it was a 'call' in the beginning, except at a deep level that something inside me just desires to till the earth!

The five marks of mission,[6] as expressed by the Church of England and developed since 1984, include a mark that is often overlooked. The fifth, 'to strive to safeguard the integrity of creation and sustain and renew the life of the earth', places Karin's expression of her ministry firmly at the centre of that which can be identified as missional activity. Karin's reflection contains a number of developments of the project which, for her, are evidence of the hand of God – Creator, Presence and Saviour. Adjacent plots were rented by a mental health unit and a woman and her special-needs teenage son, opening up opportunities for relationship-building and ministry through conversations and caring. In addition, young people became involved in the allotments, bringing them into contact with creation and opening up conversations when Karin was working her plot. Relationships grew; strawberries and raspberries grew exponentially and even the inconvenient bricks under the surface of the soil proved useful. In addition, rogation and blessing the land became a feature of the church calendar.

In Karin's words:

Experience proved that I could not use the allotment only for rest and recuperation. Conversations developed with dog-walkers or recreationalists over the fence of the park. People seemed to know that I was involved in the local church community and would share stories of illness (their own and those of family and pets), of prayer offered in traumatic circumstances and of life struggles. Stories of bereavement and new life found through Alpha courses, and healing experienced by being part of the community of people working on the allotments were also shared.

Karin's time of involvement with the allotment included a period of serious illness. At this time she found others were willing to be part of her vision for the project, which included praying for the land and for the area. Karin says:

Latterly a new helper has arrived to help – another worshipper who needed to put her seedlings into some soil but could not use her own garden. She has worked many hours and brought great talent and perseverance to the plot. She has found the work and community spirit therapeutic following huge personal trauma, upheaval and loss.

The Reader part of this story is almost invisible. I prefer to be known first, then share Jesus and lastly I may share about the church and my Reader licence. But the reason I felt called to be a Reader at the age of 34 was to be accredited and licensed to teach, share and make Jesus known. If I can do this I am content that the rest is the work of the sovereign Almighty God and the outworking of the Holy Spirit in hearts and minds.

In a formal way, there may be a future for Rogation and Harvest services. One offer of produce this year was taken to the service and then on to the local special school, building links and sharing with the local community.

However, more can be offered than thinking about services. For the future we have the hope to use the plot to grow veg and fruit for the café being planned to be built on to our church. This year we ran a pilot café project and supplied raspberries and strawberries for one of the days. I hope the plot can continue to be a therapeutic place for others: both those who dig its soil and those who eat its produce. So far it has offered many people space and helped others to find a way through trauma. May it continue to do so.

As Karin continues to take seriously the fifth mark of mission, all that motivates her and those who work with her will, in many ways, point others to Christ and the kingdom of God, fulfilling the expectation of Readers that they seek to understand the wider world and the role that the Church might have in that world.

The last three stories tell of those who spend their time walking alongside others in rather more constraining environments: hospice, mental health and prison chaplaincies. In each of these environments, sensitivity to those in the care of the particular institution is essential. Thanks are due not only to the Readers involved but to all among whom they work who have encouraged them to share their stories with us. These stories are of those who walk with others through some difficult and troubling times.

Hospice Chaplaincy

Barbara Wellman, licensed as a Reader in 1995, has been on a lifetime journey that has led her into voluntary hospice chaplaincy. Barbara relates how she was:

> raised in a churchgoing family. I had a sense of 'vocation' from my early teens, but to what? Apart from a few years at home raising small children, I practised as a solicitor for 35 years doing non-contentious family work. It was always the pastoral side of the work that I enjoyed.

After licensing, Barbara relates how she:

> ministered within an inspiring team in the same group of parishes for almost 20 years. I did the teaching and preaching that Readers do, and much else besides. I learnt to reflect theologically. I loved the busyness of it all.

Barbara learnt much of a ministry of hospitality and the offering of 'open doors' through the ministry of this church. Building on this experience and freed by early retirement, Barbara learnt about the work carried out by chaplains in many different environments. Finding herself guided towards hospice chaplaincy, Barbara says that she:

> found the new role enormously difficult at first. I struggled with 'being' not 'doing'. I envied those who had jobs to do and could attach their pastoral skills to them. I found that words – previously the tools of my trade – could be a barrier.

Silence sometimes creates a better space in which to communicate. Drawing alongside, walking with, listening, setting the world and the weather to rights, holding a hand may be what's needed. For those of faith, prayer takes many forms, and tradition – the patient's tradition – has to be understood and adopted. There are guidelines but no formulae. There are no 'right' words, other than the patient's own. There are no right answers, only good questions, and brief moments of conversation among the coffee cups and impressions left to be re-examined later. How can or should spiritual support be offered?

Many Readers report the desire for lifelong learning. Barbara, along with others who have shared their stories with us, sees her chaplaincy ministry as part of a multi-disciplinary hospice team as being 'a wonderful education'. She says that:

being part of a multi-faith spiritual support team caring for everyone has shown me that there is 'a wideness in God's mercy' (F. W. Faber) and that earth is 'crammed with heaven' (Elizabeth Barrett Browning). I feel very blessed in this work; there are moments of illumination or transformation; there is love at its heart. Perhaps that early sense of 'vocation' has drawn me slowly to this place.

Considering the institutional part of her role, Barbara acknowledges that she works:

within the Spiritual Support and Well-being team, accountable to the Lead Chaplain. As a Reader I remain within the discipline of the Church of England. I continue to try to witness to the unconditional love of God for all his creation, wherever I am. I continue to reflect theologically and prayerfully; I draw on the deep wells of Scripture. I draw on the experiences that led me to this pastoral ministry. I still lead services of evensong in local churches during vacancies and holidays.

I find myself journeying on as the role of healthcare chaplaincy evolves to meet the spiritual needs of a complex modern world. Spiritual well-being is part of holistic care for everyone; diagnosing spiritual pain is as important as physical symptoms. Spiritual support is part of the response to patient needs and choice. Since a child I have been drawn to the Bible passage that tells the story of the paralytic man being lowered through the roof of a house by his friends so that Jesus could heal him (Luke 5.17–26). I was impressed by Jesus proving that he had the power to forgive sins by demonstrating the visually more difficult physical healing of the paralysis. Now Jesus' discernment of spiritual pain is what strikes me – the man 'went home' light of heart 'praising God'. Spiritual healing is first, followed by physical and social rehabilitation. Whether of faith or not, people derive spiritual strength and comfort in time of adversity in their own ways. Strength may come (or not) through family, friends, principles, beliefs, creation, beauty, character, experience, goodness, love and from many things no longer accessible as physical or mental strength recedes. But who will 'go for us', who will keep the connections, who will walk with us? Churches are, can be, should be at the heart of 'compassionate communities' (www.dyingmatters.org.uk). Every Christian has a vocation to this unconditional ministry of friendship and sensitive good neighbourliness.

Lives seemingly nearing their end on this earth demonstrably remain full of potential for good. It is never too late to see things differently (Mark 9.2–4); it is never too late for love to blossom, for hurts to be mended, for wisdom to be shared, peace to be achieved and hope to be fulfilled. I have witnessed this. In this respect patients and their loved ones are no different from us all.

In this and other ways Barbara is fulfilling the biblical instruction to love the Lord our God and to love our neighbour as ourselves. At the same time she is realizing the fulfilment of her lifelong sense of vocation.

Hospital Chaplain

Working in a different type of hospital setting, Ross Martin was licensed as a licensed lay minister/Reader in the Diocese of Oxford in 2013. He serves as a volunteer chaplain for NHS Trust Oxford at Littlemore Hospital, Littlemore, Oxford. While Ross had intended to minister in a parish setting, he soon recognized that:

This was not to be so. I was diverted by God's insistence that I minister to patients in mental health settings. In trying to focus on what I considered to be a more traditional, liturgical LLM [Licensed Lay Ministers] role, I wasn't helped by my life experience. I had been a Probation Officer for 30 years and had an existing voluntary role for the hospital. Now, two years after licensing, my ministry involves praying with those who are suffering and who are so often also cut off from the rest of the world. Prayers with patients are mostly on an individual basis but sometimes in groups. This depends on the wishes of the patients – and their mood at the time.

Most fulfilling of all is the feeling of affirmation in every contact I experience. Many individuals are on secure lockup wards and most lead lonely, friendless and isolated lives. God invites me to reach out to them and let them know that they are loved.

You could call me a foot washer. Whatever the name, a more privileged role I can't imagine. God has truly diverted me from the parish!

Even within what might appear to be the more traditional parish part of Ross's ministry, his understanding of mental health issues has led him into a specific role ministering on behalf of the parish for a local mental health charity. Ross explains that:

This ministry involves me in running a Christian fellowship group for residents who suffer from mental health issues. We sing hymns to my guitar, have a basic worship liturgy incorporating communion by extension. I also lead a music group that meets fortnightly, which involves all of us making a lot of noise!

Often things don't work out as I have planned and prepared. Frequently individuals are stressed or indifferent. Sometimes things go wrong. In all of this uncertainty, I have learnt the great lesson given to us by Jesus' example; that perfection doesn't look like what you expect it to be. For me, just being there beside people on their journey is what really counts and I am now sure that that is what God wants of me.

Prison Chaplain

Perhaps one of the longest-established chaplaincy roles, one where the presence of a person of faith has been acknowledged as essential since an Act of Parliament in 1773, is that of the prison chaplain. This role has provided pastoral care to those denied their freedom for legal reasons ever since. While the role has changed, and the work has become established in the legislation of the prison service, the statutory nature of the work has remained. Changes in the organization of prison chaplaincy have opened up management roles to Readers in recent years. It is this role that Lisa Davies, licensed as a Reader in Liverpool Diocese in 2006, is now fulfilling. Lisa joined the Prison Service that year as a chaplain and has worked in several establishments throughout the North West. She is now the Managing Chaplain of HMP Styal women's prison in Manchester.

Lisa recounts her Christian journey as beginning, like so many, with the experience of good pastoral care offered at the time of her Gran's funeral. This experience led to Lisa's personal commitment and her own expression of pastoral care offered through Sunday School teaching and helping to feed homeless people in the city centre. Added to that was the opportunity to offer her time as a volunteer in a Young Offender Institution, giving Lisa a growing understanding of how faith and pastoral care come together.

Lisa continues her reflection on this experience of God's calling by saying:

Little did I realize that one day I would become a chaplain. I had always had a calling to work with those on the fringe of society, the people who are often isolated and vulnerable. Jesus walked alongside these very people, reaching out to the undesirables, the prostitutes, beggars, tax collectors etc. The great commission was 'to go to all people everywhere and make them my disciples'. It wasn't go to all the white middle-class people who happen to live in suburbia. God has given me the desire and ability to talk to individuals on a level, wherever that level may be, drawing alongside them and sharing the gospel message in a very direct and practical way.

The role of chaplain is never dull, you never know what you are going to be doing on any given day. The statutory duties have to be completed on a daily basis, involving visiting every prisoner upon reception and discharge and checking on their personal well-being and religious affiliation. Visiting and giving pastoral support to those in the Care and Separation Unit and those in the Health Care or Hospital Block are also part of those duties. In addition, faith-specific worship chaplains are there to support both staff and prisoners of all faiths and none. Very often we will help with family issues and have the unfortunate task of informing prisoners of the death of a relative or loved one, which is often a traumatic experience.

Being a chaplain in a women's prison is bittersweet, in so much as we have newborn babies, and often mums will bring their babies to the services for a blessing. Babies are only allowed to stay with mum up to the age of 18 months in the Mother and Baby Unit and therefore support for mum is often needed when the baby is either sent home or in some cases adopted out.

Being a Reader within the Church of England is a huge privilege and it has enabled me to work full time, ministering in a practical way to both men and women of faith and those with none. I have seen lives changed through the power of the Holy Spirit and walked alongside individuals on their Christian journey. I just thank God for the blessing of being a chaplain within Her Majesty's Prison Service.

Conclusion

In so many ways Readers are fulfilling their calling to minister in the world as well as in the Church. Stories have been told by some who teach and encourage others, walk alongside those in difficult circumstances and offer their skills and personalities in God's service and among God's people. At all times these stories reflect the desire of those ministering to share the good news with those around them, listening and meeting needs where they can. In all of these stories, though, there is a deep sense of privilege. Serving God in whatever way they are called to, those who have shared with us have also shared a sense of God's blessing as they go about what might at times seem to be very ordinary roles offered by very ordinary people. In God's world, though, no one is unremarkable.

> Truly I tell you, just as you did it to one of the least of these who are members of my family, you did it to me. (Matthew 25.40)

No wonder ministry is experienced as such a blessing by so many.

Notes

1 Blaise Pascal, 1995, *Pensées*, trans. A. J. Krailsheimer, rev. edn, London: Penguin, p. 4.
2 Gerard W. Hughes, 1985, *God of Surprises*, London: Darton, Longman & Todd, pp. 10–25, at p. 21.
3 Church of England, 2007, *Common Worship: The Admission and Licensing of Readers*, London: Archbishops' Council, www.church ofengland.org/media/41172/admissionreaders.pdf, p. 6.

4 John Whitmore, 2009, *Coaching for Performance: GROWing Human Potential and Purpose*, 4th edn, London: Nicholas Brealey, p. 10.
5 Henri J. M. Nouwen, 1997, *Bread for the Journey: A Daybook of Wisdom and Faith*, New York: HarperCollins, p. 80.
6 The Five Marks of Mission, at www.churchofengland.org/media/1918854/the five marks of mission.pdf.

4

Readers in History:
Past and Future

PHILLIP TOVEY

Books about Reader ministry repeat the story of the revival of
this ministry in 1866. Studying about ministry in North America
and the work of the Society for the Propagation of the Gospel
in Foreign Parts (SPG) led to my surprise discovery of Readers
before this date. This uncovering of a hidden story led to my
challenging the 1866 date, but while I do that in classes, candidates still repeat back to me this date as a historical certitude.
This chapter wants to question and nuance the date and provide
evidence of Readers prior to 1866. The uncovering of these stories also suggests a more missional nature of Reader ministry
then, which if connected to today might suggest a more missional nature now.

While 1866 may have been a key date in England, there is clear
evidence of Readers working in parishes in the New World and
other places before that date. The SPG, founded in 1701, sent
many clergy and laypeople around the world for mission work.
In the records, some of these laypeople are called Readers. The
word in some contexts may not have the exact same meaning as
today, but it forms the background to the modern revival. In this
early period, technically much of the rest of the world was under
the superintendency of the Bishop of London. This was only to
begin to change with the establishment of other Provinces and
the development of a colonial and missionary episcopate. So the

story is more complex than the simple repetition of a narrative of renewal in 1866. Likewise the SPG continued to use a variety of lay ministries – Reader, catechist and schoolteacher – before and after 1866, so within the society lay ministry had an important role. It is also clear that the office of Reader had a variety of meanings and uses within the SPG. This is indicative of its being a flexible category of a ministry of the Word in a variety of contexts.

This chapter intends to recover some of the stories of those involved in mission work before and after 1866 in lay ministry generally and that of Readers in particular. It is thus a story of licensed lay ministry in a wider world mission. As such this can be quite challenging to us, as the situation in England has been one of constant reshaping of Reader ministry to fit new contexts. That story also applies within a wider geographical setting. Sometimes the people are called 'catechist' but it is clear from society rules that this is the same as a Reader. These stories of Readers in mission might well inform a new vision for Reader ministry in mission and catechetical work today. The past can inform the future.

Instructions

There were 'Instructions' from the SPG that gave directions to missionaries and lay agents. For the latter the instructions drawn up in 1706 say:

> The Lay Agents employed by the society consist of schoolmasters, school mistresses, readers and catechists, two of these offices often being united in one person.[1]

This leaves open the employment of women by the Society as schoolteachers, although they don't form much of a place in the official narrative, and quite possibly were married to another schoolteacher or a clergy person. It is clear from the stories how often teachers and Readers were united together in one job, and how Reader and catechist were in fact interchangeable terms in some contexts. Samuel Seabury (see below) managed to combine teacher, catechist and Reader. 'Catechist' is a title used within the Book of Common Prayer catechism.

There are specific instructions for schoolteachers. The first is that they teach people to read the Bible and other Christian literature. Second, they are to teach them the church catechism not just by rote but by changing the heart. Then they are to teach people to be able to write. They are to use morning and evening prayer daily in the school and teach them prayers for use at home. They are to instruct people to go to church on Sunday and guide them as to the use of the Prayer Book, teaching them decent behaviour in church. They are to take opportunity to teach native peoples and black people where the possibility arises. The last statement shows that the rules are written up for the context of North America.

Catechists were seen to be those who worked among native peoples. The first appointed was in 1704. This then developed regionally; for example, due to the lack of clergy in Quebec, in 1830 the Bishop of Quebec formed a body of well-qualified catechists to teach and lead worship. This led to a strong growth in the Church. In 1866 it was agreed to have a Women's Mission Association. This promoted women teachers, primarily at first to teach to other women to promote Christian education and Christian practice. Women were later to take a key part in medical mission. It would appear that in 1866 there was not an idea that women could also be Readers and lead worship on Sunday.

This chapter will continue by giving a number of examples of Reader/catechist and their ministry in various parts of the world. This will include examples from both before 1866 and after.

Elias Neau in New York 1704

Early Christian work in New York, taken from the Dutch in 1664, is a bit sketchy, but Colonel Heathcote, who arrived in Westchester County in 1692, was concerned about the spiritual state of the people. He gave orders that his militia should appoint a Reader in every town in order that services might be held. It was harder to find clergy to serve these small congregations.[2]

The developing church in New York established in 1704 a catechizing school; this was put in the charge of Mr Elias Neau, a Protestant Frenchman who had come to New York as a trader after being imprisoned and sent to the galleys for his Protestant faith in France. He was sympathetic to the plight of slaves, black and Native American, and in 1703 suggested to the SPG that a catechist needed to be appointed to work among them. He was prevailed upon to take up the job and left his office as an elder in the French Church and joined the Church of England. He was vigorous in visiting house to house and teaching people the Christian faith. He agitated that a bill be made in Parliament to allow slaves to be baptized and catechized, which was passed. In 1712 an outbreak of violence led to some thinking that the school was subversive. The governor visited it and claimed that it was the duty of people to instruct black people in the faith. Neau was commended in his work by the governor and the council that ran New York. He died in 1722. The work was continued with the black people in New York by a variety of clergy.

Henry Barclay at Fort Hunter 1735

The son of the Revd Thomas Barclay, who lived in Albany in New York State, in 1709 Henry Barclay was directed to begin ministry with the Native Americans. Henry Barclay was born and grew up in America and was able to speak Mohawk. He studied in Yale, where he obtained an MA.[3] Then he was appointed catechist at Fort Hunter from 1735 to 1737. He then went to England to be ordained and returned as a missionary to the Mohawks. Later he was to work at Trinity Church, New York.[4] He was evidently a much-respected church worker among the Native Americans, who were extremely glad to see him on his return from England after ordination.

Here is an example of the son of a missionary continuing the work of evangelism with native peoples. One of the key gifts that he brought was his language ability, due to growing up with Mohawk peoples. The time that he had as a catechist prepared him for further missionary work. However, this should not be in any way regarded as a secondary period of his ministry. Need called him to work as a catechist, and then it called him later to be ordained. In both phases of his ministry, though, he was highly respected by the local people.

Clement Hall in North Carolina 1743

Clement Hall was a magistrate in North Carolina, somewhere the SPG was concerned about due to the lack of ordained staff sent to minister there.[5] It would appear he was born in North Carolina and stepped into lay ministry because of the need that existed. The people who had moved to North Carolina as colonists had itinerant administration from ordained missionaries, which meant that they got to see a priest only occasionally. This led to the missionary priests being involved in large numbers of baptisms and marriages whenever they visited various centres. The history of the society notes that sometimes there were 100 infant baptisms in a day due to the backlog of work.

Clement Hall would have had a ministry in leading worship using the Book of Common Prayer for morning and evening prayer and probably in teaching the catechism. Such work may seem to be simple but in places where churches are developing, lay ministers, men and women, can be fundamental in building the Church, both by gathering people together and by actually physically building churches.

Clement Hall comes to the focus of history when in 1743 he approached the SPG with the wish now to be ordained. As there was no bishop in the American colonies he had to travel to England for this, a fairly long and hazardous journey in a sailing ship. However, he returned and faithfully worked another 12 years as one of the few clergy people for hundreds of miles. He says he travelled 14,000 miles, preaching 675 sermons and baptizing in all 6,195 people in his itinerant phase. In 1755 he was appointed to a settled mission and died in 1759. It is said that he baptized 10,000 persons in his ministry.

Often today people feel the call to lay ministry through a clear need set in front of them. Clement Hall saw the need for leading some basic worship and teaching. It was his fruitful years as a Reader that prepared him for ordained ministry. The development from Reader to ordained ministry happens today but some people who are Readers are not always generous in their welcome to someone who goes on to get ordained. However, there are many excellent priests who had a formative experience by being a Reader, and this should be celebrated and welcomed.

Samuel Seabury in Huntingdon 1749

Born in North America in 1729, Samuel Seabury was the son of a minister, who sent him to Yale in 1744. Halfway to the completion of his first degree he began to lead services in places where there was no clergy person. He also began to preach in private homes and churches in the vicinity. He began one particular work in Huntingdon, where people came to faith and suggested building a church. At this point he was still 18, and the congregation approached the SPG for aid. He was thus appointed as catechist at Huntingdon from 1749 to 1752. His role was to read morning and evening prayer on Sunday and use printed sermons instead of preaching himself. He also catechized the children of the parish. He worked for a while as schoolmaster at Oyster Bay, perhaps hoping that the society would give him additional income. He also supplemented his income with a practice in medicine. The aim was to save money for the trip to England for ordination and possibly for further medical study in Edinburgh.[6]

Because of the future episcopal career of Samuel Seabury, his life is particularly well researched. It shows that the work of what we would call now a Reader was often the action of young men prior to their ordination. In this case Seabury was too young to be ordained, and probably didn't have the finances to be able to travel to England. But his work as a catechist enabled him to prepare himself for his future ministry. In our terms it would be a part-time post, giving him free time to raise more money and do further study. This is beginning to sound like some of the sandwich courses that have been developed in our own time.

Fogo in Newfoundland 1817

The Revd J. Leigh visited Fogo in 1817.[7] There he found a small church with services regularly performed by an old man of 87. This man had a salary of £15 from the government. This was the first visit of any clergy person to the island. However, Leigh found that the children had been validly baptized by this old man. Thus a very quiet ministry had occurred of leading worship and baptizing by this layperson.

While this unnamed person was technically not a Reader, the SPG particularly employed lay agents in Newfoundland. In 1821 it developed measures for the appointing of catechists or school-masters in its outstations. They had three functions: conducting schools; reading the service; reading sermons on Sunday. As such they performed the functions of a Reader on Sunday but also had an important connection to the work of the schools. The link between a Reader and a teacher was seen to be helpful in these remote areas.

Demsy Jordan and Mr Anderson in Nova Scotia 1818, 1821

Demsy Jordan was a 'native Reader', part of a group of black people who had escaped slavery in the United States to settle in Tracadie, Nova Scotia. He ran a flourishing settlement and built a church and school. He had a ministry of encouraging people in their Christian faith and practice. Jordan had a long ministry, dying at the age of 89 after 20 years' blindness.[8]

It is clear from the report on this ministry that the words 'catechist' and 'Reader' are used interchangeably. There appear to have been considerable numbers of settlers in the area, and the church used laypeople in their evangelization.

In 1821 we find a Mr Anderson at a colony of highlanders in Remsheg. He was the schoolmaster at Merigomish but also acted as a catechist explaining the Scriptures to the colonists. Part of his talent in doing this was that he could translate sermons into Gaelic.[9]

William Jackson in Barbados 1818

Born in Barbados in 1811, William Jackson was to have a distinguished career, eventually becoming a bishop. He made great progress in school and became headmaster at the age of 18. He was confirmed by the first Bishop of Barbados and at the age of 17 was licensed as a catechist. He was assiduous in church work and was ordained deacon in 1834, then becoming the minister of parishes in Barbados, Trinidad and St Vincent.[10] He left Barbados in 1879 and died in Ealing in 1895.

While we only have a brief outline of this man's life, and the majority of his ministry was ordained, we see again – and this time outside of Canada – the importance of a schoolteacher and catechist being combined. As such he would have had to lead worship and catechize people, preparing them for baptism and confirmation. For some, such ministry was a life's work; for others, their calling changed to move into ordained ministry. William Jackson started as a Reader and went on to have a distinguished ministry in the West Indies. Perhaps one of the notable things in this story is the age – 17 – at which he was licensed. It would appear that the colonial church could spot talent and at times be flexible enough to give young people responsibility within the Church.

Joseph Bird in Sea Cove Newfoundland circa 1850

Another story comes from Newfoundland, through the travels of Bishop Edward Field. He used a church ship to get around a number of very small and remote fishing communities. Indeed, he used the ship to hold services in places where there were no churches. He discovered the church in a fairly poor state. In Sea Cove a father brought his three children to be received by the bishop after lay baptism. When questioned about the baptism itself the reply was that it had been done by one Joseph Bird, 'and a fine Reader he was'.[11] Charles Pascoe notes other cases of baptisms by the father as the head of the family or by a midwife. He notes that lay baptism was common in Newfoundland and Labrador, and might be performed by a clerk or the captain of a vessel.

Here we uncover a new dimension of lay ministry. The absence of clergy was such that baptism by laypeople, normally only occurring in an emergency, had become the norm. Joseph Bird got the job because he was able to read. He was more educated than other people around, and able to do the service in the correct way. In one way he was not a Reader in the technical sense but in another he exhibits some of the charisms of the office: being educated and able to lead worship.

While sacramental ministry is not the norm for the office of Reader, it is always possible that in emergency there may be the need for either baptism or for extended communion (not possible in 1850). Once again we see a layperson stepping forward to perform what was necessary for their community, in this case the Christian baptism of their children.

Joseph Leycester Lyne 1859

Somewhat closer to home, the office of catechist or Reader was still occasionally used. Joseph Lyne was to become one of the monastic pioneers of the Catholic revival. At the age of 18 he went to Trinity College, Glenalmond, then a leading Scottish theological college. Leaving the college at 21 he was too young to be ordained deacon. He was given a job as catechist in Inverness for two years with the Scottish Episcopal Church before he could be ordained deacon.

Baroness de Bertouch called the office 'catechist'.[12] Peter Anson called it 'Reader'.[13] Whatever the exact terminology to be used, it is clear that he was employed in a lay capacity for a couple of years in a role of teaching and preparing people for baptism. There is clearly some conception of a Reader in the Scottish Episcopal Church at about the same time it is being discussed in England. Joseph Lyne went on to become Father Ignatius of Llanthony, having a very controversial life as a Benedictine monk and evangelist in the Church of England.

Ranchi in Bengal 1869

The mission work in the district of Ranchi in Bengal resulted in small Christian communities in over 300 villages. The district was divided into 35 circuits and in each of those a Reader or teacher was stationed. Thirty-two chapels and several houses for Readers were built by the mission. They led the worship, preached the gospel and did some basic Christian teaching, using the Book of Common Prayer translated into the vernacular. Missionaries travelled round baptizing and leading Holy Communion. From 1869 to 1870, 533 converts were baptized, and in 1870, some 268 persons were confirmed. This growth led to opposition from Hindu elders. Nevertheless the church continued to develop, and a 'native pastorate' was begun in 1837. In 1886 the Uraons (or Kurukh), a tribal people, were trained as catechists to work among their people. This mission strategy was developed in other parts of India.[14]

So the strategy was to have settled Readers and teachers who were from the local people in every district, who would then minister to the Christians in their villages, and also to have missionaries who would itinerate around these circuits and perform a further teaching and sacramental ministry. The Reader was a more local ministry and the missionary an itinerant one. In this arrangement there are shades of Methodism and of multi-parish benefices. There is even an element of Reader house-for-duty in this story.

Hawaii 1889

In 1794 King Kamehameha I appealed for Christian missionaries to come to the islands.[15] Visiting explorers such as Captain Cook and Vancouver had discussed religion and introduced European ways in agriculture. In 1819 the King's successor broke the taboo and destroyed local idols. In 1820 American

Congregational missionaries arrived. Kamehameha IV made a direct appeal to Queen Victoria for English missionaries, and the Church of England consecrated a missionary bishop, who with two priests travelled to Honolulu, arriving in 1862.

By 1889 the situation in Hawaii had changed considerably. There had been a large influx of Japanese and Chinese people to work on the islands as labourers on sugar plantations. In 1889 the congregation in Honolulu began to contribute to a part-time salary for a Chinese Reader to work in church planting. The aim of this project was to develop a church for the Chinese community, both as a group of people and as a physical church. This was a successful project and within three years one of the congregation, Woo Yee Bew, was ordained deacon. It is not clear from the report if this was the person who was the Reader.

Here a Reader is involved in church planting. The cause for the church plant is in part linguistic and to do with the changing ethnic situation in Hawaii. As people migrated, so the need developed for new initiatives in mission to work with people of a different linguistic and ethnic grouping. Putting in a part-time salaried Reader seems to have been a very effective strategy, in that evangelization and a physical church were established quite quickly.

This is one of a number of cases where Readers have been employed in church planting. They have also been used in other contexts where a full-time church worker is needed but not necessarily a priest. A flexible ministry such as that of the Reader does not always have to be a voluntary one and can be stipendiary.

Titus Zwane and Mr Crosby in South Africa 1895

A further mention of a Reader occurs in the history of the evangelization of Tongaland in South Africa.[16] In 1881, Titus Zwane, a 'native catechist', laboured for a year to begin missionary work in the area. This was followed up in 1895 with an expedition to Tongaland by the Revd C. Johnson, who managed to meet the queen. The report of the visit aroused interest in mission in Tongaland. One problem was the selling of European drink to the local people, which had caused a lot of alcoholism.

A trader challenged Johnson on the lack of zeal to take the gospel to an untouched area. The trader was a Mr Crosby, who then made himself an example by becoming a Reader in the most remote mission post established in Zululand.

The details about these two persons in the story are sparse. Sometimes a 'native catechist' has a ministry not unlike a Reader. Their basic role may be to run a parish that does not have a clergy person, leading the people in worship (morning and evening prayer) and in teaching people the catechism. There may have been little difference between the work of Titus Zwane and Mr Crosby. However, in both of them there can be seen a zeal for taking the gospel to places where it has as yet been unheard. In both cases this seems to have been stronger than in the clergy. Preliminary surveys of new work, followed by a mission action plan, can fully include a variety of lay ministries, in this case catechist and Reader. Zeal for mission can and should be a part of a vision for Reader ministry.

A Survey 1841

In 1841 *The Foreign Missionary Chronicle*, an American Presbyterian publication, conducted a survey of numbers of missionaries and other staff, including catechists.[17] This looked at a number of different denominations and it is clear that catechists were not limited to the Anglican churches. It does, however, give a rough indication of the number of catechists employed by mission societies in that year: in India the SPG employed seven catechists and the Church Missionary Society (CMS) 132. The CMS has one catechist in South Africa, 18 in New Zealand and 41 in the West Indies. This is not to suggest great accuracy for these figures, and there is a dearth of information on the SPG; however, the survey shows that both of the major Anglican mission societies were employing catechists prior to 1866, and indeed that this was a wider movement.

It is clear that the employment of catechists or Readers, both as overseas missionaries or as local missionaries, was an important part of mission strategy in the nineteenth century. The numbers varied considerably, but they could be extremely effective in the mission of the Church. The question is to what extent this overseas experience led to the revival of the office in the Church of England. Did overseas Readers lead to home Readers?

Reflections

This chapter is not intended to be a complete survey of lay ministry in the eighteenth and nineteenth centuries. However, it has aimed to furnish enough information to suggest that there was the equivalent of Readers in parts of what is now the Anglican Communion prior to 1866, and that at that time some of these areas would have been seen as a part of the Church of England.

There are, however, various trends that can be seen in these stories. The very title 'Reader' has a number of aspects to it. One is simply to be able to read, which was an important ability in a time when many people were illiterate. It is intimately linked to the ability to read the Bible and the Book of Common Prayer. A priority was given in missionary work to the translation of those two books. This led to another aspect of 'Reader', namely the ability to read in different languages. Such ability led to the employment of local people as a part of the mission of the Church. In remote areas laypeople step forward to read the services. This even includes in some places the practice of lay baptism. It is clear that in such remote places as Newfoundland there was a community acceptance of older people who could read leading services and baptizing children. This is church growth from the roots upwards.

There is also a fascinating interaction between Reader and catechist. Teaching children the Christian faith was part of parish work in the Church of England, but in other parts of the world a catechist might well teach both children and adults. One of the classical aspects of Anglicanism was to use the catechism in preparation for confirmation. Sometimes this involved the employment of 'native Readers' and it is probable that their local roots enabled them also to be involved in evangelization. However, the employment of European catechists in mission work was also not unknown.

There is also a link between a catechist and a schoolteacher. The rules of the SPG show that there was a certain degree to which schoolteachers were to take a spiritual lead and teach godliness in terms of manners and church attendance. Teaching, Christian profession and Christian praxis were all seen as part of the role of a schoolteacher. The linking of these offices can be seen in Samuel Seabury's early work.

Zeal of the mission was not confined to the clergy. The rebuke of the trader in South Africa led to the expansion of mission, partially led by laypeople. This evangelistic role was also a part of the catechist/Reader ministry. Local catechists had the big advantage over the expatriates of knowing the local culture and language.

There can be seen a shading of different types of story between lay 'ministry', lay 'ministries' and a lay 'minister'. In these three words a gradual progression of lay work can be seen. Lay ministry is a general calling of all people. In the stories, we see in remote parts that some colonists desired to meet to pray or to have their children baptized. Laypeople stepped forward in the absence of clergy people to begin to perform some of their actions. Gradually a set of ministries developed: reader; cate-chist; schoolteacher. These are more formalized but may be still quite diffuse and voluntary. They can, however, become more formal still when a particular layperson is identified to one of these roles as a lay minister. The SPG from its beginning had a conception of lay ministry.

There is also a question of call. In some places, need led to the stepping forward of a layperson. This was not an office com-missioned by the Church but would have to have community support in order for it to be viable. In other places, support came from the local church, where a congregation paid for a layperson to be their catechist and do outreach. In other places the cate-chist was supported by the missionary society or appointed by the bishop. Gradually the place of the missionary society was to fade out and episcopal appointment became the norm. So we see a progression: community support; congregational support; and then episcopal support and approval.

Pointers

These stories are about the missionary zeal of the Church. Laypeople stepped forward to partake in the mission of God and in some places were highly influential in that role. This is not to deny a partnership with ordained ministry but it is to make sure that the lay voice in history takes its rightful place. The stepping forward in mission of laypeople in some places clearly precedes the arrival of clergy.

The place of the Reader in mission in the past was clearly significant. It is unfortunate that some people talk about the 'church of maintenance' and the 'church of mission', as if the former were never interested in mission and the latter is where it is all happening. Biblically and theologically, the Church must be involved in mission, and there cannot be a church of maintenance that is not interested in mission and still be an acceptable vision of the Church. It is also unfortunate that some people see the office of Reader as connected to the church of maintenance and not of mission. This clearly does not represent a view that expresses where many of the current lay ministers in Reader ministry are at. Mission has to be at the heart of Reader ministry as much as of any other ministry. These stories from the past should point us to a future in which Readers take up their missionary past and are revitalized by the call of the gospel. Readers are people of mission.

With an eye on the past this can be sketched out a little more clearly. Readers and catechists were involved with evangelization and the preparation of adults and children for baptism (and confirmation). There is still a vital role in this ministry today. Enquirers' groups and Christian development groups should be at the heart of Reader ministry. But there are also other areas where the past directs us to the future. Cross-cultural or cross-linguistic work was an important part of Reader ministry. Many Readers, because of work, are required to know other languages. Readers could be in the forefront of opening congregations in different languages, to attract people from around the world who have begun to settle here or are living here for a few years as part of their work. With the growing cultural diversity of England, there is big scope for congregational development where English is not used as the language of worship. There is a corollary to this in that Readers may be taken by their work to live overseas for a period of time. This is another mission opportunity, and the place of Readers in the past in primary mission should encourage their role in such mission today. Laypeople are not trained to be Readers only in the Church of England, but their training is portable around the world.

We have also seen an intimate link between Reader and teacher. This has perhaps not been so strong in the Church of England in recent times. However, the Church maintains a lively interest in education in general and religious education in particular. There is a big role for Readers, as educated laypeople, to be involved either in religious education, in assemblies or in after-school clubs. It would be wonderful to see a movement of lay chaplains who are reader–teachers in every church school and in many of the state schools. While not being able to be as prescriptive as the SPG directions for schoolteachers we see above, the role of gentle commendation of the Christian gospel to the young people of society is an absolutely essential part of the mission of the Church today in this land.

The story in India of the strategic role of Readers in the evangelization of the countryside continues to be a narrative that is of importance here. The model developed in India was of Readers being housed and having a number of villages to oversee with an itinerant clergy person who came along and did sacramental ministry. This sounds increasingly like a Methodist circuit or a multi-parish benefice. Readers clearly have a strategic part in country ministry, requiring a particular style of collaboration between the lay and the ordained. This story could inform mission action planning to see Readers not as second best – 'We would prefer a priest but will put up with a Reader' – but as integral and vital to the mission of the Church. As yet house-for-duty Readers are not common, but that does not exclude their development in future.

The needs of the Church led to laypeople stepping forward into leadership. The lack of clergy led to alternative strategies that depended on the use of laypeople and lay ministers. This is not only a story from the past but also a story for the present. It does not have to be seen as a failure of the Church in the lack of priests but as requiring a more holistic vision of ministry and mission that integrates lay ministers with those who are ordained. History suggests that we need this more holistic view.

Notes

1 C. F. Pascoe, 1901, *Two Hundred Years of the S.P.G.: An Historical Account of the Society for the Propagation of the Gospel in Foreign Parts, 1701–1900. Based on a Digest of the Society's Records*, vol. 2, London: Society for the Propagation of the Gospel in Foreign Parts, p. 844.

2 H. P. Thompson, 1951, *Into all Lands: The History of the Society for the Propagation of the Gospel in Foreign Parts, 1701–1950*, London: SPCK, p. 71.

3 Pascoe, vol. 2, p. 855.

4 C. F. Pascoe, 1901, *Two Hundred Years of the S.P.G.: An Historical Account of the Society for the Propagation of the Gospel in Foreign Parts 1701–1900. Based on a Digest of the Society's Records*, vol. 1, London: Society for the Propagation of the Gospel in Foreign Parts.

5 Pascoe, vol. 1, p. 24.

6 B. E. Steiner, 1971, *Samuel Seabury, 1729–1796: A Study in the High Church Tradition*, Athens: Ohio University Press.

7 Pascoe, vol. 1, p. 93.

8 Pascoe, vol. 1, p. 116.

9 Pascoe, vol. 1, p. 117.

10 Pascoe, vol. 1, p. 215a.

11 Pascoe, vol. 1, p. 99.

12 Beatrice de Bertouch, 1904, *The Life of Father Ignatius, OSB, the Monk of Llanthony*, London: Methuen, p. 69.

13 P. F. Anson, 1955, *The Call of the Cloister: Religious Communities and Kindred Bodies in the Anglican Communion*, London: SPCK, p. 52. See also C. Walker, 1864, *Three Months in an English Monastery: A Personal Narrative*, London: Murray and Co., pp. 22–5.

14 Pascoe, vol. 1, p. 497.

15 Pascoe, vol. 1, pp. 460–8a.

16 Pascoe, vol. 1, pp. 344–5b.

17 Western Foreign Missionary Society and Presbyterian Church in the USA, Board of Foreign Missions, 1841, *The Foreign Missionary Chronicle: Containing a Particular Account of the Proceedings of the Western Foreign Missionary Society, and a General View of the Transactions of Other Similar Institutions*.

5

Readers as Pioneers?
Might Pioneer Ministry Help
Church of England Readers to
Re-imagine Their Ministry?

GRAHAM DODDS

Introduction

Over the past few years a new category of official role has emerged in the Church of England – pioneer ministers. Evolving through a period of intense interest in mission in the Church as a whole, pioneer ministry is presented in two forms, ordained and lay. What each carries as a responsibility is to be involved in the setting up or sustaining of a fresh expression. The term 'fresh expressions' was first used by the report *Mission-Shaped Church*,[1] which was noted by the General Synod of the Church of England in 2004. A fresh expression of church is explained, according to the Fresh Expressions website, as:

a way of describing the planting of new congregations or churches which are different in ethos and style from the church which planted them; because they are designed to reach a different group of people than those already attending the original church. There is no single model to copy but a wide variety of approaches for a wide variety of contexts and constituencies. The emphasis is on planting something which is appropriate to its context, rather than cloning something which works elsewhere.[2]

In 2005, provision for the discerning, training and supporting of pioneers to work in fresh expressions was considered by the Church of England as a whole in a consultative process. From the responses to the consultation, while support was given to the proposals, there was also concern that pioneers should not become a separate category of ministers. This was for a number of reasons:

- Dioceses structure their patterns of authorization and training for lay ministry generally in a range of ways and it is therefore very difficult to graft a new national 'category' on to this varied pattern.
- There was concern lest the new life emerging in fresh expressions of church and associated ministries was stifled by undue regulation.
- There was a concern that the Church may be moving too quickly to set up national frameworks without allowing appropriate time for organic development.[3]

Readers are cited, in the same commentary concerning pioneer ministry on the Church of England website, as people who can exercise a pioneer ministry without needing to be licensed further; pioneers are generally licensed as lay workers. Numbers are not huge as yet but anecdotal reports suggest they are increasing, and how the ministry will emerge into the future regarding their standing in the panoply of official ministry categories is of course yet to be determined. However, it might be noted that the inception of pioneer ministry stands within a backdrop of some dioceses reviewing, renewing and redefining their definition of a Reader's role. This redefining process has not been an official movement, but over the past 15 years some dioceses have favoured a different title for Readers, namely 'licensed lay ministers' (LLM).

My purpose here is to explore how Readers might be a part of pioneering ministry (if that is the way their vocation directs them) and to ask further if there should be an official Reader pioneer category in the Church of England (as there are ordained pioneers and lay pioneers) and what training might be appropriate for Readers who tend towards a pioneer ministry. To do this I shall consider what pioneering is about, offering my take on the theological basis behind pioneering and how this compares with Reader ministry. From a recent conversation with a Reader who is involved in local pioneer work, and some detail from other Readers active in my diocese, I will comment on how this ministry is shaping up locally. I will finally trace a little of the history of the training of Readers over the past two decades, how it is tending towards a pioneer trait, and pose some questions that might be relevant if a diocese, area circuit or other constituency wants to consider how its Readers or lay preachers might train to exercise pioneer ministry.

What is pioneer ministry about?

A tradition has built up over the past 20 years, for those responsible for training Readers and more recently licensed lay ministers in the southern province of the Church of England, to meet at Sarum College in Salisbury each year for a conference. Although, as I said, the annual gathering has generally attracted those in southern dioceses, gradually other dioceses and Methodist areas have found it helpful. At the last gathering I and one of my colleagues led a discussion on the nature of pioneering work and achievements. It is from this discussion, among others, that I draw some of these insights.

I began by asking what pioneering is in broad terms. When we think of pioneering work in secular terms we might think of great scientists who have broken through a barrier to develop new technologies or industry or medicine. Others are involved in social pioneering work and have made life conditions better for huge swathes of the population. We might think of those responsible for alleviating some of the poverty in the world, bringing better education to young people or adults, caring for the ageing population and enabling people to have more affordable lives through family planning. All these kinds of pioneers are engaged in putting their original ideas into practice for the common good. Originality seems to be at the foremost of their work. They have an idea that few others have thought of and they make it happen.

Indeed, I was privileged some years ago to interview Dame Cicely Saunders, the founder of the modern-day hospice movement, for a published Lent course entitled *Communities of Hope*.[4] My colleague and I journeyed to St Christopher's in Sydenham to speak with her. What she said about the benefits of the movement was really interesting and formed the text to promote discussions for home groups meeting during Lent. Yet also the way she achieved the promotion and implementation of this incredible movement was fascinating. It appeared to me that she had an enormous compassion combined with an intellect and practicality that made the movement dynamic and robust. But tempered with these qualities she showed that she wasn't so determined that she was inflexible. Her ability to learn and her intention to set about learning was so apparent and inspiring in her story. She used the now famous term a 'community of the unlike', meaning that she deliberately or intuitively met with people who were very unlike each other in order to strengthen the project. That takes skill, honesty, courage and a high degree of emotional intelligence to make it happen. She almost seemed to possess a sixth sense that detected the way forward.

At the Sarum Reader conference I used this insight as an example to ask what pioneers do and what they need to be in order to be pioneers. People chose their own pioneer and offered their thoughts: pioneers are entrepreneurial, sometimes angular, sometimes difficult to work with, original in different ways, exciting, determined, caring but not always in a conventional way, insightful, innovative and provocative. The descriptions that emerged made me think of the prophetic gifts God endows. Often the prophets described in the Bible have similar characteristics. Indeed, the prophetic ministry of God seems to me to be what pioneers and the movement towards pioneering is founded on. So how do we understand the role of prophecy in today's Church?

One of the best ways to look at the prophetic ministry, in my opinion, is through the work of John Henry Newman, because Newman used his remarkable comprehension of ecclesiology to place the prophetic ministry among two other ministries, those of priest and king. The three offices of Christ are an ancient way of considering the ministries of the Church, first signified in the Old Testament and then fulfilled in Christ. As the Gospel writers and Paul note in their descriptions of the nature of Christ, these three offices become fundamental for the ecclesiology of the Church. Through the Holy Spirit they are the gift of God to the disciples of Christ in every era. The French Roman Catholic theologian Yves Congar, influenced greatly by Newman, uses them to define the role of laypeople in his seminal work, *Lay People in the Church*.[5] Congar suggests that it is the prophetic office of Christ that is the imperative specifically of the laity. And in Newman's *Sermons, Bearing on Subjects of the Day* the prophetic gift is described as 'deep reflection and inventive genius', with the result of leading the Church into innovative and exciting new worlds.[6]

If pioneer ministry is a term closely related to prophetic ministry then careful thought about how to train people who are given this vocation will be essential. For some leaders and members of the Church this attention will be motivated by a further desire to grow the Church. But care must be taken here because more often than not the growing of the Church will be a by-product of the prophetic ministry, not the sole purpose of it. I detect that there has been, in recent years, a subliminal debate in some areas of the Church of England as to how to order what became known as the Archbishop's quinquennial goals:

- Growing the Church.
- Re-imagining ministry.
- Contributing to the common good.[7]

Archbishop Justin Welby continued the work towards the goals, and dioceses debate them at various levels of church governance. One of the debates is around the order in which they should be placed. Most people see 'Re-imagining ministry' in the middle but 'Contributing to the common good' is seen by some as coming before 'Growing the Church', whereas others place the latter firmly as the first priority. In some ways it may not matter which goal takes priority over the others; however, as the two goals are different the confusion is not always helpful.

Pioneer ministry, in the way it is presented, fits more with the notion of contributing to the common good of society. If the Church is shaped around this contribution to society then surely it will have knock-on shaping effects for the model of exercising lay and ordained ministry. This could provide a re-imagined ministry. Some have even suggested that church growth should not be a priority at all but an outcome of the Church's contribution to the common good. There are others, however, who wish to promote growing the Church first, with the outcome of a contribution to the common good. Yet when pressed, church growth is a very difficult thing to define. For example, should it be by numbers in attendance? Per week? Per month? Per Easter and Christmas attendance? Per percentage of the population? Or should it perhaps be by numbers of baptisms, marriages and funerals? By home-group members? By influence in the local area in schools, industry, retail and so on? Or yet again should it be by involvement of church members in local bodies such as parish councils, social agencies and so on? If Church growth is prioritized then often this will be taken to mean attendance at the regular Sunday service and fellowship. But as is experienced in many places, this is declining while other weekday events are rising in numbers, such as cathedral weekday services and messy church and after-school clubs.

Returning to the Reader trainer conference at Sarum, one of the things a number of people remarked upon was that pioneers can't be trained. They are born with an ability, a gift to innovate. What is needed is space for the exercising of the gift, and that can be tricky, for the Church is not ideally set up to keep innovators. We need only look in the Anglican Church at people such as John Henry Newman and John Wesley to see how they found themselves fighting their corner. It may be that the Church needs to reshape its ecclesiology not only to cope with, but also to encourage, the prophetic gift of God within its midst.

Even if pioneering is a gift given by nature, what can be nurtured are the skills useful to make the initial ideas of a pioneering ministry begin to emerge as practicalities. Just as leaders need managers so that their leadership is supported and sustained, so pioneers need support that will enable the projects they engage in to flourish. However, I wonder sometimes if there are too many managers in the modern-day Anglican Church, with fewer leaders than necessary to sustain the dynamic of a growing Church.

Originality

Many of the group of Reader trainers suggested that a degree of originality was present in the pioneering work they considered.

A medical scientist might discover a cancer-busting drug or an astronomer a new comet, examples of originality many people consider as the popular use of the word. However, there are other ways of being original.

Cicely Saunders' 'community of the unlike' was a means of support and development that had an air of originality. The multi-disciplinary group that examined ideas around palliative care monitored trajectories of thinking for the hospice movement and created synergies so that the movement took shape. The originality here is in using something that is known already (gathering a group of unlike people) and focusing them on a contemporary subject (researching palliative care).

There are pioneers who may not seem quite so innovative yet they still remain pioneers, for their originality rests in applying known ways of doing things to new situations. For example, a social scientist may take a social theory and apply it to a new context. If the bringing together of the theory and the context has never been done before, then the originality lies in the configuration of it – in a unique synergy. In the work I engage with in my diocese I see people taking known ways of being Church and applying them to new contexts. It's not original in one sense, yet it is in another.

Before looking at some practical examples and asking some questions about training in the skill of pioneering, I want very briefly to explore what lies at the heart of pioneering ministry.

What are the components of a pioneering ministry?

At its heart, I want to suggest, pioneering engages in a prophetic ministry. For me the three offices of Christ – prophet, priest and king – lie at the heart of all ministry. The Catholic theologian Avery Dulles expresses it like this: 'As a worshipping community, the Church is priestly. As a community of thought and education, it is prophetic. As an organized society equipped with governing functions, it is regal.'[8] Pioneer ministry appears to me to resemble prophetic ministry the closest. Pioneers seem to be people who are exploring and pushing out the boundaries, leading from the known to the unknown, in a famous educational dictum. So it is under this title that I would like to explore something of the theology behind the gifting.

Wendy Allen, in her doctoral thesis on Newman's offices of Christ, proposes a definition of what is at the heart of the prophetic ministry. Through an in-depth reflection on the office of prophet in Newman's work she concludes that it involves three central roles:

- Responsibility for the development of Christian doctrine;
- Discovery of means of contextualization and application of revelation;
- Provision of varied views necessary for education and teaching.

In her examination she states that the prophetic role should be exercised in two environments. The first is in community, in the sense of individuals undertaking creative work, and the second is in the whole Christian community, through a corporate *phronesis* (a Greek word meaning the wisdom of practical thought) instinctively rejecting falsehood and affirming truth. She agrees with Newman that clergy and laity might breathe as one (Newman terms it *conspiratio*) as they take part in this office as the whole people of God. Also, each office has its own intrinsic authority, derived from the infallible nature of revelation, to 'guarantee the truth of genuine development against spurious speculation and error'.[9]

Combining Allen's three components above with Newman's previous description, that of 'deep reflection and inventive genius', this now gives a clearer view of what is involved in prophetic ministry. In summary, it is a deeply reflective and inventive expression of the context, doctrine and ongoing educational needs of the contemporary world. As for the environment of the pioneer/prophetic ministry, it is exercised in the local and corporate communities of the Church. This may not be the final

definition of pioneer or prophetic ministries, or even a very pragmatic one, but it does express something of the theology that
undergirds it.

How does a definition of the role of Reader fit with pioneer ministry?

If, as suggested above, the role of pioneer is essentially prophetic, then I suggest that the definition of a Reader's ministry
can be interpreted quite closely to incorporate the components
of a prophetic ministry. The national guidelines,[10] issued by the
Ministry Division of the Archbishops' Council, interpret Canons
E4, E5 and E6 to mean that: 'The primary duties of readers are
to preach and teach, and to conduct or assist in conducting worship.' This is complemented by a further paragraph that states:
'Readers assist in the pastoral, evangelistic and liturgical work of
the Church in the parish or area where they are licensed.'[11]

Most dioceses interpret this national definition of Readers in
their local context, although as will be seen, much is still held in
common. I am grateful to my colleague the Revd Jennifer Cole,
who works with me in the Reader Studies department in my diocese, for compiling some definitions from diocesan websites for
the conference. They pertain to dioceses in the southern province
of the Church of England as the conference was largely attended
by these dioceses. They are as follows:

Diocese of Oxford – Readers are known as licensed lay ministers. Readers are laypeople in the Church of England from all
walks of life who are called by God, theologically trained and
licensed by the Church to preach, teach, lead worship and assist
in pastoral, evangelistic and liturgical work.

Diocese of Guildford – licensed lay ministers (Readers) are
laypeople who are trained and authorized to lead worship and

preach in church; they also engage in pastoral work, outreach and service in their communities.

Diocese of Winchester – the ministry of LLMs (formerly called Readers) is essentially one of preaching, teaching and leading worship within a pastoral context.

Diocese of Portsmouth – a Reader is someone who is called by God, selected and trained by the Church and licensed by the bishop to exercise a ministry primarily of preaching and teaching, and leading worship. A Reader is a layperson who, in a special way, works collaboratively with parish clergy and the congregation in modelling and building up the ministry of the whole people of God.

Diocese of Salisbury – a licensed lay minister (LLM) is a lay man or woman who has the bishop's licence for a preaching and teaching ministry within the parish where he or she lives or works.

Diocese of Bristol – licensed lay ministers (LLMs) are usually local people who are key members of their congregations, exercising leadership in worship, mission, pastoral care and prayer. They will often be active members of the PCC, leaders of home groups or Bible-study groups and well integrated into the local community. They are representatives of the Church in the life of the community and reflect the light and love of Christ wherever they are.

Diocese of Bath and Wells – Readers are lay ministers who are called to lead services, preach and attend to pastoral work arising from these ministries.

Diocese of Exeter – see 'Bishops' Regulations for Reader Ministry'.

Diocese of Chichester – Readers are laypeople, called by God, trained and licensed by the Church to preach, teach, lead worship and assist in pastoral, evangelistic and liturgical work.

Even given that websites can be out of date and the definitions may have changed somewhat, what it shows clearly is that dioceses have the liberty to interpret locally what work and ministry a Reader is involved in. Indeed, this is acknowledged in the Bishops' Regulations. What lies at the heart of their ministry, above and beyond other lay ministries, is the ability to preach sermons. Some dioceses have introduced lay pastoral assistants to complement and assist the work of the parish priest in the pastoral responsibility within the 'cure of souls'. Some dioceses have also introduced ministries such as lay worship assistants, which normally means a layperson trained to lead Services of the Word. Yet in order to hold a licence to preach regularly, many dioceses limit this to those who hold the Reader's licence, as distinct from the other ministries a Reader might be engaged in, such as conducting worship and ministering pastoral care.

So Readers have opportunity through their licence to engage in six disciplines: preaching; teaching; conducting worship; pastoral work; evangelistic work; liturgical work. In each of these, given Allen's definition of prophetic work above, there is at least the possibility of being a pioneer to find either original ways of engaging in the disciplines or applying known theory to the particular context of ministry in the discipline. To make the theoretical statements, argued above, more practical and clear, the next stage in the discussion presented here is to consider how some Readers are engaged in pioneering work from reflection on their own stories.

Stories of Readers' pioneering work

Canon Melvyn Matthews, in an article produced for Bath and Wells Diocese on collaborative ministry,[12] described the Church as having two categories of laity. Laity A, as he described them, keep the local church cogs turning. They are the PCC, the house-group leaders, the churchwardens, the flower arrangers and so on. Without this committed group of workers the church as a place of worship, learning and fellowship or as an organization would not exist. However, Laity A must not obscure Laity B, who are those who are attempting to live out faith in the community. They can sometimes be seen as on the fringe of the church in that they often only attend worship and don't get involved with the 'inside' tasks and jobs. Laity B are being salt and light in the world and need the oasis of worship, fellowship and learning groups for support. However, their vocation lies outside the church walls.

In the Old Testament, God called a particular tribe to look after the worship and liturgy. There is the need for this in the present-day Church, yet at times it feels like that is the entirety of the Church. What the following three stories demonstrate is that there are some who are called particularly to this kind of Laity B pioneering ministry and mission.

In 2015 my colleague and I asked Readers in our diocese to take part in an exercise to tell us how they ministered in the communities they serve, as opposed to the church work they undertook on Sundays. Approximately 10–15 per cent of all the Readers responded with a paragraph or two or in some cases a page of description. Here is a flavour of what was described:

Jim Loring writes:

I have worked for a retail bank for 37 years and from time to time organized Bible studies and prayer meetings. Two years ago I started a weekly lunchtime Bible study and there are now between 10 and 15 participants dialling in by teleconference. The summary of the talk is distributed by email to 150 colleagues from different Christian traditions as well as those who have no church background. The topics have a work-related theme and have included studies on Gideon, Evangelism and the Gifts of the Spirit. Too often church teaching and activity relates to parish ministry and overlooks the fact that we are called to live a distinctive lifestyle 24/7. My vision is to help Christian colleagues to live out Christ's values in the workplace and be exemplars in demonstrating the bank's values. I am encouraged by these words of Jesus to Paul from Acts 18.9, 'Do not be afraid; keep on speaking, do not be silent. For I am with you, and no one is going to attack and harm you, because I have many people in this city' (NIV). We're now praying for the creation of more local groups and for internal signposting of our informal network.

Meg Hill writes:

From its inception I have been involved with Somewhere to Go (STG) on the committee level. STG is a day centre for people who have drug, alcohol, mental health or housing issues. When I retired, nearly 11 years ago, I started as a volunteer. I found, to my surprise, that I often got into conversations about God and Jesus. STG is a busy place with people coming in needing all sorts of practical help, and I felt frustrated that there was never time for the conversations about Jesus to have any meaning. A volunteer started who had spent many years in and out of prison, but one night God visited him in his cell and his life was never the same again.

Together we decided to look into having another day, independent of STG, where we would offer hot drinks, a meal and then, for those who wanted to stay, we would sit round the table with tea and biscuits and have a discussion about Jesus and what he can do in our lives. And so The Beacon was born nearly 10 years ago. My co-founder, Tommy, died of cancer nearly two years ago but The Beacon keeps going and there are always people who want to stay for the 'Jesus' time. God continues to bless us with money and volunteers. Our aim is to have volunteers cooking and putting the room ready who themselves are vulnerable, which can be quite a challenge. However, we do see them growing so much through this trust put in them. God in his goodness always provides us with reliable Christian people as well. I don't feel I am any use as an evangelist but I have all sorts of chats with people that I would never otherwise have known and through them sometimes get drawn into conversations that it is a privilege to be a part of.

Stephen Rymer writes:

I was first licensed on 27 April 1995 in the Cathedral Church of Holy Nativity, Ndola, Zambia, by Bishop Jack Cunningham (who later became a local vicar to me for a short time until his death). I am a member of a small group called Use-less, Share-more. We are a collection of 'odd-bods' with a concern for our local society and for the future of creation. We meet monthly over a shared meal and plan local events, such as working parties to keep local footpaths clear, an apple-pressing day, an any-questions event with our prospective candidates for the next parliament. Over the past five years we have initiated the formation of two other community groups: The Allotment Association and the Eat Cary Community Garden.

What I find interesting about these three examples is the diversity of pioneer spirit. For Jim it is in starting something he has felt deeply about. I know he has shown determination and commitment over the years and his scheme owes its existence, in part, to his entrepreneurial skills. Meg has developed ideas in community as part of a wider group of people, then branched out into a new possibility with The Beacon enterprise. Stephen has 'pioneer' written throughout his work in every area and demonstrates how to be pioneering in the ordinary things he has taken part in. From the other responses we received, most fell into this latter category, where Readers are taking the everyday activities of Reader ministry and attempting to be pioneers in undertaking them. This suggests differing ways of approaching pioneering.

I asked Stephen if I could discuss with him further what inspired his work in the community, and whether he had always had this vocation:

Graham: Stephen, when you wrote to me, you felt that you had always been a pioneer. What do you mean by that?

Stephen: It came about because the beginning of my ministry was being a Reader in Zambia. So I arrived in Zambia as an engineer and almost immediately was met by people from the church. And within a month or six weeks or something, I was singing in the choir, on the PCC, and was drawn into something about Reader training. And a small group of us would meet a couple of times a month for about a year and then the bishop licensed us as lay Readers. We were set free but there was such a need. Immediately I was doing radical things. So I vividly recall, very soon after being licensed, two of us being sent out to a big church with the reserved sacrament to take the Sunday morning communion service, and preach, and distribute communion.

When we came back from Zambia I was living in rural Ayrshire, in Glasgow and Galloway Diocese, and again there were quite a number of little congregations scattered around with very few ministers; we got very involved in running an interregnum in a very big church and I was hardly trained.

Graham: And who gave you the permission to do this?

Stephen: The Bishop of Glasgow. I went to see him and took my old Zambia licence with me – just as well I did because at the end of the conversation he said, 'I think you should carry on. Have you got your licence with you?' – which I had. I gave it to him and he countersigned it and that was my authority.

We then came back to rural Gloucestershire, a village congregation and a very open priest there who allowed a lot of
things to happen. So we started a youth group and I remember
asking him if the kids could do something in church on Easter
Sunday morning. Could we construct a tomb in front of the
altar? And that was allowed to happen. I have no idea now
what battles he had to fight but there was a lot of freedom.

Looking back I feel as though a lot of my ministry has
been about trying to make religion relevant, connected, real.
The latest way of doing this is the Iona community. One of
the things that attracted me to Iona, apart from the style of
worship, is that as a member there of the community you are
accountable to the other members in your local community
for all aspects of your life as a Christian. It has a structure that
makes you think all the time of how you are leading your life,
not just at Sunday worship, but all the rest of the time.

Graham: What do you think sustains you as a pioneer?

Stephen: Being able to work some of those things out in my
local benefice – helping with worship and the café church.
I have always read a lot – all kinds of things, edgy things.
I'm really grateful to people who have pointed me to books –
sometimes religious, sometimes more secular ones. Over the
years I have tried to maintain morning prayer on my own.
Sometimes that has worked, sometimes it hasn't worked so
well. Nowadays my wife and I pray, read the Bible, talk about
it for a bit, pray together each morning. That's been much
more satisfactory – doing it with somebody else.

Graham: Do you think you can train to be a pioneer?

Stephen: I think you need to be a particular kind of person. I heard yesterday that one of my exploring Christianity
group has gone to see the archdeaconry warden about pioneer ministry. And I can see that she has that certain aptitude
for reaching out, getting involved with Street Pastors or the
café church. So I think it does need a certain type of person

and the opportunity to experiment with it. That seems crucial now, looking back on it. It's a sort of apprenticeship – being allowed and supported to do things that are different. I have always felt called to be on the boundary of the Church; it's always been about pushing out of it and making things more real, connected.

Among the many things that emerge from these stories and the interview is the need to find space to experiment, the permission to try things out, the support of those in authority and the inner discipline to sustain such work. In some ways pioneering begins with a kind of playfulness, as John V. Taylor described in his seminal book on the Holy Spirit, *The Go-Between God*.[13] Rowan Williams also discusses the stage of being free from responsibilities in order to find responsibility. In the first chapter of his *Lost Icons*, speaking of the space children need to play, he says:

> children need to be free of the pressure to make adult choices if they are ever to *learn* how to make adult choices. For them to be free for irresponsibility and fantasy, free from the commitment of purchasing and consuming, is for them to have time to absorb what is involved in adult choice. Failure to understand this is losing the very *concept* of childhood.[14]

Training

I conducted a survey of Readers in the Diocese of Bath and Wells in 1998, which asked questions about how Reader ministry had changed in the light of the changes in training that had taken place. The movement from a variety of training pathways to a single course, constructed by each individual diocese, shifted the support and indeed the actual style of Reader ministry from dependence to the beginnings of interdependence, from adult–child (vicar–Reader) to adult–adult (church leader–church

leader). By that I mean that whereas in the past the Reader
tended towards being the vicar's little helper, the style changed
to the Reader becoming a member of the leadership team. In the
past the Reader was stereotypically ushered into a room to sort
out the rotas for preaching and leading, or even simply handed
a rota to work to. By the end of the decade the nature of collaboration was tending towards a meeting of vicar and Reader
as team.

The Reader expected to pray with her or his incumbent, to
work together on challenges, to use their transferable skills
to aid the work of ministry. They also expected in return for
the vicar to offer professional support through appraisal and
review, through the offer of further training – perhaps going
to Continuing Ministerial Development together. The adult–
child relationship was beginning to wane, to be replaced by
an adult–adult response to the needs of ministry within the
parish or benefice.

What caused this change, at least in part, was the change in
training provision. Before 1989 there was little real regulation
for the training of Readers. While it was true that some Readers
were made to write assignments to fulfil a kind of general ministerial exam, the practice across dioceses was varied and random.
One example I found was of a Reader who had met the warden of Readers over an evening sherry and after the discussion
was put forward for licensing. Another, in the same diocese,
was of a GP who had completed some 50–60 essays on doctrine, pastoral care, the Bible, church history, ethics and much
more. The bizarre and irregular nature of the training regimes
did not go unnoticed, and in the late 1980s, Reader wardens
asked the National Training Officers for Adult Education,
Yvonne Craig and Hilary Ineson, to provide some help. What
they devised with others was a moderation scheme, which
would moderate initial Reader studies and report nationally.
This continued throughout the 1990s and up to approximately

2006/7, when it was finally concluded. What replaced it, in the light of the *Formation for Ministry within a Learning Church* report in 2003,[15] is a periodic external review every six years, with annual self-assessment. This is administered through the Regional Training Partnerships.

The scheme in my diocese has evolved through this period of 20 years to equip Readers for their ministries. What has changed is the Church of England's ambition for mission. With the Decade of Evangelism, the *Mission-Shaped Church* report and the introduction of fresh expressions and pioneer ministry, questions around how to provide training for this are emerging. The Church Missionary Society (CMS), with its Director of Mission Education, Jonny Baker, alongside the Church Army (CA) are at the forefront of this training and it may well be that those who feel called to Reader ministry, but with a leaning towards pioneer ministry, would do well to seek ways of blending learning with the excellent CMS and CA[16] resources and methods. However, there is also the need to include in every Reader scheme the principles of good pioneering, which from the CMS website are about groundbreaking, transforming and sustaining mission.[17] Certainly the Church needs to embrace these principles. Too often the Church has replaced transformation with service. It is one thing to serve others, and rightly so, but Jesus' ministry was also about transformation.[18]

It may also be useful for those responsible for Reader studies to seek a partnership with the fresh expressions course, mission shaped ministry (msm).[19] In the UK and abroad, msm has been run many times and affords the student a year's reflection, resource and experience of mission projects.

This all begs the question of whether it is possible to train pioneers. In some ways the answer is 'no' and in some ways, 'yes'. If pioneering is a gift – 'a gift of not fitting in' as the CMS website suggests – then that is not necessarily something training can offer as a skill. However, understanding how not to fit in, yet achieve what is necessary for the mission of God, might suggest skills of discernment, how to shape ideas, emotional intelligence, formation of spiritual courage, people skills and learning how to find personal and professional support in a support group. Yet in their hearts I suspect pioneers are born not made. The Church of England has criteria for ordained pioneer ministers, and in 'Forming and Equipping God's People for Mission and Ministry', produced in May 2014, it suggested that Reader ministry was 'in flux', and that more needed to be done on the criteria for mission, implying that pioneer ministry might be the way forward for Readers in mission:

> The nature of Reader ministry is in flux. Many Readers have been equipped for ministries that include preaching, teaching, leading worship, taking funerals and exercising pastoral care. In some cases this has resulted in a loss of focus on mission and ministry outside the church and in an unhelpful clericalisation of the role. The Ministry Council's priorities recognise the need for a shift:
>
> 'Traditional forms of lay ministry such as Readers need a transforming change of direction towards the teaching of faith both in catechetical work and apologetics.'[20]

However, what follows in the document does not demonstrate the distinctiveness of pioneer Reader ministry. If there is to be an integration of Reader training with pioneer training, then perhaps this needs to happen, and ways of blending Reader and pioneer ministry training could both reinvigorate and re-align it with national goals.

All these issues raise some questions that may need answering before the Church can really encourage the formation and sustaining of Readers being pioneers. And if this is true at the national level then it is also true for a local church or diocesan and area scheme.

So what is needed if this is going to work?

An overarching question concerns the philosophical and perhaps the ontological question of what Readers and pioneer ministers are. Can Readers also be pioneers? Are pioneers a distinct category of minister? The Church often likes to categorize ministers in order to see how to train them; and in fairness, when there are often large sums of money exchanged as training courses are bought to train people for official roles, clear definitions are helpful. Looking at the epistles, Paul and others introduce the Church to a list of ministries, such as evangelists, teachers, pastors, helpers, administrators and so on. Yet it is important to remember two things about this plethora of giftings. The first is that, in my opinion, it's not exhaustive; and the second is that we can exercise more than one ministry. Today I shall be involved in designing and shaping a governing body for Reader ministry in the diocese – that will emerge from my teaching role. This afternoon I shall see a couple for marriage preparation – a pastoral role. Likewise, Readers will possess the gifts to be Readers, but that will not be the sum total of their gifts. It may well be that they have a pioneering spirit as well, as was seen in the stories above.

On the other hand, pioneer ministry can be seen as a separate category of official role in the Church. The advantage this provides is that a discrete training programme can be employed to encourage focused learning for the outcome of pioneer ministry.

It is important and pragmatic to discuss and reach a conclusion about this because a successful pioneer ministry candidate will be granted a lay worker licence or, if pursuing the Church Army route, will become a Church Army officer, which will enable her or him to apply for pioneer roles in dioceses. The licences are nationally accepted, but a local diocese and bishop will need to appoint the person to a parish, benefice or area to work. The Reader licence is slightly different. Although the licence is nationally accepted in the Church of England, it is prone to various degrees of interpretation and configurations of ministries held within it, and some will be more evangelistic, some more pastoral.

The distinction between being a pioneer minister and a Reader with the potential of pioneer work as part of the role description is a little like the difference between deacon and priestly ministries. Although they are highly related, there is more emphasis on an evangelist's ministry in the deacon and more emphasis on the presidential role within the eucharistic community in the priest. Perhaps the pioneer ministry with its concern for fresh expressions of Church might emphasize the evangelistic ministry, the Reader ministry might assist the building up of the body. What the term 'Reader pioneer' might be suggesting is that we loosen these categories to offer a more human, whole and realistic provision of leadership. Whichever way it is seen, and that is for local agreement and policy, it ought to be noted that we are talking about differences in ministry and charism and not status. Well-established ministries such as Readers have the opportunity to be enhanced and complemented by pioneer ministry, not threatened by it.

So it is important to be clear about whether Readers can become pioneers as part of their Reader ministry or whether a diocese or area might want candidates to choose between training to be a pioneer minister or a Reader. If Readers can embrace the concept of being a pioneer as part of their ministry, then a second question arises as to how to train them incorporating elements of pioneer ministry. As I have suggested earlier, it may well be worth investigating how pioneer training components already established in places such as CMS and the Church Army and other places might be blended into the learning.

However, before doing that it may be worth thinking through how the various marks of the Church – one, holy catholic and apostolic – will be balanced and represented in the training scheme. In other words: how the training scheme can help Readers be pioneer liturgists and preachers for a ministry on Sunday and weekday worship; how they can be trained to be pioneers in building up the fellowship of the church through house groups and social occasions in their teaching and pastoral ministries; how the training scheme will cover a mission emphasis, perhaps using the insights gained from pioneer training.

As well as the consideration of the balance of the scheme, a further question might be raised with regard to recruiting potential Readers who may have the pioneering spirit. My experience has been that people who are pioneers are often people who are on the edge of the Church. This can mean that the demands of an increasingly involved procedural process for entering official ministries can be a trial for the budding Reader pioneer. However, ways of making the process more accessible will also need to ensure that Disclosure and Barring Service (DBS) and safeguarding processes are complied with, to avoid unnecessary problems further down the line.

Another set of questions are to do with the integration of Readers who feel called to an 'in-church' ministry alongside those who find themselves wanting to engage in pioneering work outside the Church. Training incumbents need to be aware of the diverse nature of ministers across the Church and that some will conform to 'Laity A'-type work and others get excited about 'Laity B' (see 'Stories of Readers' pioneering work' above). I put it deliberately like that, using the words 'conform' and 'excited', because that is often how it can come across, as though one ministry is conformist and another much more exciting. The apostle Peter gets big churches in Rome and epistles named after him while his brother, Andrew, is remembered towards the end of November, if he's lucky. Like the description of the Prodigal Son's return, it's easy to honour the more colourful ministries, neglecting the more everyday ones. So care might be necessary in guiding training incumbents and congregations who have within them both pioneers and more traditional Readers.

One final question is about support. When my colleagues and I began to think about the new category for the Church of England's ordinand and curate training, namely Initial Ministerial Education (which was named IME 1–7, now IME phase 1 and IME phase 2), I asked colleagues: 'What about IME 8–10 (IME phase 3)?' What I meant by 8–10 was the period of three years immediately after the curacy had ended. This is often a period of new challenge in learning what it is to be an incumbent, chaplain or associate minister. In Reader training the period after licensing is crucial to form good habits of supervision, professional development, continuing spiritual formation, extension of skills, knowledge and so on. One of the best ways to do this is through workshops and action learning sets for particular stages and focuses of ministry. Especially with a new ministry, or category of ministry such as pioneer ministry, the people who know most about it are the practitioners. An action learning set is a group of people who come together from time to time to discuss their own agenda in relationship to their calling. In our diocese, the groups I have convened of those who are concerned with Readers as pioneers have resulted in very fruitful conversations.

Conclusion

If the Church is to survive then it is clear it must value many diverse and sometimes new forms of ministry and mission. The Church of England has called its people to re-imagine ministry. There are clearly questions about how this might happen and Readers need to make their voices heard in the discussion. Pioneer ministry is an exciting possibility and those who are promoting it must be careful not to integrate it into the mainstream of the Church too early, if it is not to lose its edge; and even then, when it is part of the nationally recognized ministries, it must be allowed its freedom to grow. It is equally early days for the possibility of Reader pioneer ministry and, in my opinion, there must be time for Readers to experiment as pioneers, in a safe place, before establishing whether this will become a norm for the future. Indeed, if pioneer ministry is not just a bridge to the next form of Church, which I believe it is not, but a fully integrated form of ministry provision, then the dynamism of a potential Reader pioneer ministry could benefit the Church as a whole. It could marry what is already established with new insights and be a re-imagined model for all lay people, fully prophetic, fully spirit-led, fully supported and monitored, fully accountable, and set free to be what God is calling the Church to be.

Notes

1 Mission and Public Affairs Council, 2004, *Mission-Shaped Church: Church Planting and Fresh Expressions of Church in a Changing Context*, GS 1523, London: Church House Publishing.

2 www.freshexpressions.org.uk/about/introduction.

3 www.freshexpressions.org.uk/sites/default/files/Encouraging lay pioneer ministry.pdf.

4 R. Bowman-Eadie and G. Dodds (eds), 1998, *Communities of Hope: A Lent Course*, London: Darton, Longman & Todd.

5 Y. Congar, 1957, *Lay People in the Church: A Study for a Theology of Laity*, London: Bloomsbury Publishing Co.

6 J. H. Newman, 1844, *Sermons, Bearing on Subjects of the Day*, New York: Appleton & Co., p. 63. To consider a wider exposition of the three offices, see M. Davies and G. Dodds, 2011, *Leadership in the Church for a People of Hope*, London: T. & T. Clark, pp. 63–7.

7 In the General Synod presidential address of November 2010, Archbishop Rowan Williams adopted three goals, which became known as the 'quinquennial goals' – see http://rowanwilliams.arch bishopofcanterbury.org/articles.php/919/archbishops-presidential-address-general-synod-november-2010. Note, however, that what the Archbishop said at the presidential address was not how the three goals eventually were interpreted. To note them when they

evolved, see www.churchofengland.org/media/1782970/gs 1895 – quinquennium goals update.pdf.

8 A. Dulles, 2002, *John Henry Newman*, London: Continuum, p. 110.

9 W. K. Allen, 2005, '"Prophet, Priest and King": An Evaluation of John Henry Cardinal Newman's Model of the Church', University of Bristol: Unpublished PhD thesis, p. 117.

10 These are found in the Bishops' Regulations for Reader Ministry www.churchofengland.org/media/1543345/bishops regulation for reader ministry.pdf; or Ministry Division, 2000, *Bishops' Regulations for Reader Ministry*, London: Church House Publishing.

11 Ministry Division, *Bishops' Regulations*, p. 7.

12 Diocese of Bath and Wells, 1996, *All in it Together*, Wells: internal publication.

13 J. V. Taylor, 1972, *The Go-Between God: The Holy Spirit and the Christian Mission*, London: SCM Press.

14 R. Williams, 2000, *Lost Icons: Reflections on Cultural Bereavement*, Edinburgh: T. & T. Clark, p. 27; emphasis in original.

15 Working Party on the Structure and Funding of Ordination Training, Archbishops' Council, 2003, *Formation for Ministry within a Learning Church. The Hind Report*, GS 1496, London: Church House Publishing.

16 www.churcharmy.org.uk/Articles/417599/Our_work/Training _and_Vocation/How_will_we.aspx.

17 http://pioneer.cms-uk.org/wp-content/uploads/2013/03/cms_ pioneer_prospectus1.pdf.

18 For more on this insight about the Church and its role of service provider and transformer in society, see J. Drane (2008), *After McDonaldization: Mission, Ministry and Christian Discipleship in an Age of Uncertainty*, London: Darton, Longman & Todd, pp. 101–4.

19 www.missionshapedministry.org.

20 Ministry Council, May 2014, 'Forming and Equipping the People of God for Mission and Ministry', p. 13, quoting 'Transforming Ministry: A Statement of the Ministry Council's Current Priorities for Ministry', March 2014, p. 8 – www.churchofengland.org/clergy-office-holders/ministry/ministerial-education-and-development/initial-ministerial-education.aspx.

6

Postscript

PHILLIP TOVEY

The journey of this book has been to try to take a fresh look at Reader ministry with the conviction that this is a highly significant ministry for the Church of England. In the book we have used story quite considerably, either from interviews with individuals today or by looking at journals of historical people. Phillip has wanted to qualify the 1866 date with the suggestion that Readers go back further, to 1706. Both Sally and Phillip have looked at the theology of Reader ministry with different lenses in order to bring out fresh approaches. Sally, working from the bottom up, has creatively used some categories of new monasticism to characterize the ministry. Phillip has had a debate with the work of John Collins and set Reader ministry within a baptismal ecclesiology. Some historical work has suggested a key part for Readers in catechetical work, schooling and church planting. This challenges us all to think of Readers in the aid of mission and as agents of God's mission in the world. Graham developed this in his chapter on the relationship between Readers and pioneers, picking up some of the hints in early documents that have been insufficiently explored.

As we write this book, a committee has been set up to look at lay ministries in the Church of England and produce a report as part of the re-imagining-ministry agenda. We hope this book may contribute to that report but suspect that the timetables of each may not enable dialogue in depth. Preliminary discussion has kept one eye on the Roman Catholic document from the

USA, *Co-Workers in the Vineyard of the Lord*,[1] which develops a baptismal ecclesiology and then distinguishes between ordained ministry and lay ministries. Unlike in the Church of England, there are not some canonically defined ministries such as church-warden, lay worker, and Reader. Thus the Catholic report discusses a variety of ministries, including those within music, the education of children, as well as pastoral workers in the Church. Through Roman Catholic canon law there is a clear distinction between these people and any religious involved in such work, who are seen to have a distinct consecration. Catholic theology also gives a clear distinction between lay and ordained ministry. However, it is a helpful report and it is quite clear that in the Church of England the ministry of Reader sits alongside other lay ministries, more formal and informal, and some dioceses have their own ecclesial ministries, such as pastoral visitor, evangelist and minister of extended communion. While this book has focused on Readers, there is no attempt to squeeze out these other ministries or undermine ordained ministry. The focus at the moment is on the fostering of vocations to all types of ministry, lay and ordained.

The growth in different types of lay ministry and of lay workers has also been noted in the Methodist Church. The report *Lay Workers in the Church* notes the changing context of lay ministry and its growth in Methodism.[2] It did not, however, discuss the relationship of this to that of lay preacher. A variety of lay ministries also exists in the Reformed tradition and in the Orthodox churches, as can be seen on their websites.

There is a degree to which there is an element of déjà vu in the present discussion about discipleship and lay ministries. There were significant reports on this in *All are Called: Towards the Theology of the Laity* (1985) and *Called to be Adult Disciples* (1987) and *Called to New Life: The World of Lay Discipleship* (1999).[3] Other reports have noticed the development of diocesan ministries, including the 'Formal Lay Ministry Report' (1999) and

'Authorised Lay Pastoral Ministry' (2002).[4] The proliferation of these ministries has also been noted in *Order in Diversity* (1993) and in *The Mission and Ministry of the Whole Church* (2007).[5] Alongside this could be reports that call for the recognition of evangelists and lay pioneers, and others writing to suggest a recognition of lay celebrants for funerals.[6] There is as yet a lack of a common mind as to what lay ministries are needed in the Church as a whole and the shape that these particular ministries might take across the dioceses. *Read Upbeat* does show that some Readers are threatened by this diversity,[7] but in one way this is more to be seen as an opportunity where Readers can foster vocation and help train people in particular lay ministries. It is perhaps to be expected that in the future a variety of these types of ministries will continue to develop and flourish, and it should be remembered that sometimes the experience of ministry in a small area leads to a growth and a calling to a canonical ministry such as Reader.

So what of the future of Reader ministry? The authors set themselves a task to look at what they might be saying 50 years in the future. What might we say if we were writing a similar book, but at the two-hundredth celebration of Reader ministry in the Church of England? Here are some of our thoughts.

Sally says:

From my point of view the best thing we did when we were reconsidering ministry throughout the Church of England 50 years ago was to acknowledge the leadership potential already contained in the body of theologically educated licensed lay ministers who we called Readers. So many people, we discovered, had professional skills that were not being utilized by the Church. Our network of local churches meeting for prayer and fellowship and sharing food and possessions together in a way that has proven to be so powerfully countercultural would not have existed without the acknowledgment of those Readers who were natural leaders. Readers, alongside their priest colleagues in their newly configured oversight roles, have brought the teaching of faith through actions and words back to life in the country as well as in our cities. They have been unafraid of the challenges involved in combining their deep spirituality and theological understanding with their embeddedness in the world of work and social action. It was Readers who turned the Church inside out and who have given much in the service of their communities in the name of Jesus Christ.

Graham says:

I am so pleased that what we did, 50 years ago now, was to release Readers from their Sunday duties and encourage them in their chaplaincy-type roles. They have become the leaders of mission for many local churches. The lay worship leaders are doing a great job in devising creative and imaginative worship. As well as that it was a real insight of theirs to concentrate their work on the partnership of the Church with church and community schools. Fewer people would know what the good news of Jesus Christ is if they hadn't spent the long hours working with young people and children in after-school clubs and fellowship groups. And our decision as a Church to give them permission to celebrate Holy Communion with their local Christian communities in homes has meant that the priestly ministry has rightly found its proper episcopal role and the Church now truly embraces a eucharistic theology.

Phillip says:

When we ceased to see Readers as a problem and looked at trained laity as an opportunity, things began to change. The stressing of the role of vocation development and training other laypeople led to a release to work with laypeople in the church and in the community. Some took this up with in particular the vision of mission and pioneering and developed churches in particular niches. Vocational work led to more people becoming Readers but also a greater diversity of what they were doing. Much of the local mission in terms of nurture groups and outreach to particular areas became conducted by the ministry team with Readers taking an equal part in that work. Their role in mission increasingly became central to the Church.

Thus this book is not the final word and sits in an evolving history of Reader ministry. The fact that this ministry has grown and developed is something to be celebrated. God still clearly calls many people to this canonical office. It has significantly grown since 1866 and it is one area that particularly needs consideration for flourishing. As people who work alongside many Readers, we are committed to enabling that to happen for the good of the mission of the Church.

Notes

1 United States Conference of Catholic Bishops, 2005, *Co-Workers in the Vineyard of the Lord*, Washington: USCCB.
2 Methodist Church, 1995, *Lay Workers in the Church*, www.method ist.org.uk/.../co_lay_workers_in_the_mc_1995rep_0907.doc.
3 Working Party of the General Synod Board of Education, 1985, *All are Called: Towards a Theology of the Laity*, London: CIO Publishing; Board of Education, 1987, *Called to be Adult Disciples*, GS 794, London: Board of Education; Board of Education (1999), *Called to New Life: The World of Lay Discipleship*, GS Misc 546, London: Church House Publishing.
4 Internal Reports in the Ministry Division.
5 ABM, 1993, *Order in Diversity*, ABM Ministry Paper No. 5, London: General Synod; Faith and Order Advisory Group, 2007, *The Mission and Ministry of the Whole Church: Biblical, Theological and Contemporary Perspectives*, GS Misc 854, London: General Synod of the Church of England.

6 House of Bishops, 1999, *Good News People: Recognising Diocesan Evangelists*, London: Church House Publishing; Fresh Expressions, no date, *Encouraging Lay Pioneer Ministry*, www.freshexpressions.org.uk/sites/default/files/Encouraging lay pioneer ministry.pdf.; Alan Stanley, 2015, *The Challenge of the Funeral Celebrant: A Mission Opportunity for the Church*, Grove Worship W 224, Cambridge: Grove Books.

7 Ministry Division, 2009, *Reader Upbeat: Revised Report*, www.readers.cofe.anglican.org/u_d_lib_pub/p112.pdf.

Index of Names and Subjects